Halloween

STEVE RUSSO

HARVEST HOUSE PUBLISHERS
Eugene, Oregon 97402

Cover design by Terry Dugan Design, Minneapolis, Minnesota

HALLOWEEN
Copyright © 1998 by Steve Russo
Harvest House Publishers
Eugene, Oregon 97402

Library of Congress Cataloging-in-Publication Data

Russo, Steve, 1953–
          Halloween / Steve Russo
                p.   cm.
          ISBN 1-56507-851-9
          1. Halloween.   2. Amusements—Religious Aspects—Christianity.   3. Chris-
          tianity and culture.   I. Title.
GT4965.R87   1998
394.2646—dc21
                                                                                    98-5765
                                                                                    CIP

Printed in the United States of America.

01   02   03   /BP/   10   9   8   7   6   5

Table of Contents

Acknowledgments

This book is truly the result of many people working in close cooperation.

I begin with a word of appreciation to my friend, Neil Boron, host of the "Lifeline" Program on WDCX in Buffalo, New York. The initial idea for this book came during some "off air" conversations we had when I was a guest on the show two years ago.

Of course, where would I be without all my friends at Harvest House Publishers? They have earned my gratitude for believing in the potential of this project. Many people contributed their talents and encouragement to this book. In particular, I am grateful to Bob Hawkins Jr., LaRae Weikert, Carolyn McCready, Ray Oehm, Betty Fletcher, Julie Castle, and Teresa Evenson.

A special word of appreciation to Dr. Robert Saucy, from Talbot Seminary, for giving the project a review through the eyes of a theologian. I learned much from him while a seminary student and continue to appreciate his input in my life.

My most special thanks, as always, go to my family. My wife, Tami, has again proven to be a tireless source of emotional strength and support for me personally. Of course, my children, Tony, Kati and Gabi, have been affected by my time spent writing; however, they have been nothing less than encouraging the whole time.

And finally my hope is that this book will honor my Lord and Savior Jesus Christ and be a blessing to His people.

PART ONE

A Historical Perspective

I

Halloween Then and Now

Many parents, especially those with small children, face the dilemma every year of what to do about Halloween. Most thoughtful Christians wrestle with celebrating this holiday because of its apparent connections with the occult. However, since it is such a popular holiday in our culture, there is great pressure to conform. In order to make a solid decision on what should be done with Halloween, it is important to step back and examine its true origins. We will also look at how the early church responded to the celebration of Halloween and the way it is currently celebrated in our own culture.

Halloween Then

Halloween has its ultimate origins in the ancient Celtic (Irish, Scottish, Welsh) harvest festival, Samhain (pronounced *so-wen*), a time when people believed that the spirits of the dead roamed the earth. The Celts adopted Druid beliefs and customs, in pre-Christian days, to commemorate the end of summer and the last day of the year.

As the power of the sun waned with the onset of winter, people were afraid that life itself, and not just the year, was coming to an end. They imagined that the night was haunted by ghosts and witches, and more particularly by the spirits of the dead who were revisiting their earthly homes. With the supernatural rampant, the night was full of danger and omens. Concerned for their survival, people employed every possible means to fortify the flames of the dying sun and to chase away, or at least pacify, the evil spirits. For this purpose they lit bonfires and sometimes offered gruesome sacrifices.

The Celtic New Year, November 1, is also the beginning of the new year for wiccan witches. The first day of November was also the Day of the Dead, a time when it was believed that souls of those who had died during the year were allowed access to the land of the living. It was a time when people believed that spirits were wandering the earth as well.

The festival Samhain was related closely to the season of the year: a time when crops should be harvested and animals brought in from distant fields. All of a farmer's crops and livestock needed to be secure for the hard winter weather to come. In other words, by Halloween, what is vulnerable should be protected and whatever is not protected is fair game for the elements. The first day of both the new year and winter were seen as a point of transition in the annual calendar. In addition, many beliefs and rituals were associated with this day. The gates that separated the worlds of the living and the dead (this visible world and the world of the spirits) were opened. This barrier between the two worlds was brought down, and the souls of those who had died during the year were allowed entry to the other world where they once lived.

Some said that bonfires were lit on Samhain to light the way for wandering spirits while others said the fires were lit to keep spirits away from people's homes. With the belief in the wandering spirits of the dead came the custom of preparing offerings of special foods and of dressing up as these spirits and wild animals. These customs were widely practiced in ancient Ireland, which was converted to Christianity largely through the initial efforts of Saint Patrick in A.D. 300–400.

Christian missionaries then began a redefinition of calendrical celebrations. To a large extent the early church adopted and accommodated the traditional religious beliefs and practices of those it sought to convert. Many of the festivals and holidays observed today resulted from this policy and were derived in some part from already-existing festivals and celebrations. The first day of November was declared All Saints' Day, and later November 2 was proclaimed All Souls' Day. The celebration began at sundown prior to November 1.

Many traditional beliefs and customs associated with Samhain—most notably that night was the time of the wandering dead, the practice of leaving offerings of food and drink to masked and costumed partyers, and the lighting of bonfires—continued to be practiced on October 31. This day became known as the Eve of All Saints' Day, the Eve of All Hallows' (the term "hallow" refers to saints), or All Hallows' Eve. It is the glossing of the name Hallow Eve that has given us the name Hallowe'en.

All Saints' Day was designated by Pope Gregory IV in A.D. 835 and was placed on the early church calendar to pay honor to all the saints who did not otherwise have a feast day reserved for them. About A.D. 900 the church recognized that All Saints' Day had not supplanted the pre-Christian customs, so in an attempt to get closer to the original intent of the festival it declared November 2 as All Souls' Day.

November 2 was set aside in recognition of the souls of all the faithful departed who had died during the previous year. The church also redefined the belief that the spirits of

Samhain, once thought to be wild and powerful, were now said to be evil as well. It was also maintained that the gods and other spiritual beings of traditional religions were diabolical deceptions. It was taught that spiritual forces that people experienced were real, but they were manifestations of the devil—the prince of liars—who misled people toward the worship of false idols. Thus the customs associated with Halloween now included representation of ghosts, skulls, and human skeletons (symbols of the dead), the devil himself, and other malevolent evil creatures such as witches.

With the onset of the Protestant Reformation, which most historians credit Martin Luther with spearheading on October 31, 1517, the church holidays diminished in importance. This then opened the door for holidays like Guy Fawkes Day in England (today a bigger holiday than Halloween) as well as the Day of the Departed and the Day of the Blessed Souls in Latin America. The connection to early celebrations is still there, but in addition to being vehicles for expression of personal, social, and cultural identity, these celebrations now also reflect broad historical currents.

Even after Christianity had succeeded in suppressing paganism, people continued to practice some of its customs. However, they reinterpreted them to give them new and somewhat innocent meanings. Going almost to the other extreme, they transformed a fearsome night into an occasion of jubilation, especially for young people and children.

Halloween Now

Halloween was and still is one of the most important festivals of the year throughout Ireland and Scotland. Many popular games are played by children, such as dunking for apples in a water-filled basin or bobbing for treacle-covered apples suspended from a string. Then there are the special foods like oat-based breads, sowans and barnbrack, and potato pudding. Fortune-telling tokens such as rings, buttons, thimbles, and coins baked into one of the special food dishes are also quite popular.

The divination practices, various pranks, and bonfires associated with Halloween night in Ireland and Scotland are still preceded by a week of children going house-to-house disguised with blackened or false faces and fancy dress, carrying turnip lanterns to beg for money, fruit, or nuts. In some areas the activity for this week is called "Halloween Rhyming," with the children chanting this chorus:

> Halloween is coming! The geese are gettin' fat;
> Please put a penny in the oul' man's hat.
> If you hinnae got a penny a haep'ny,
> then God bless you and your oul' man too.[1]

Halloween has been known in North America since Colonial days. But it wasn't until Irish settlers brought their Halloween customs (which included bobbing for apples and lighting jack-o'-lanterns) to America in the 1840s that the festival started growing in popularity.[2] By the middle of the twentieth century it had become mostly a children's holiday. But by the late 1970s there was a great resurgence of Halloween adult activities. In the last decade it has exploded in the United States as a national, highly commercialized holiday. Take a look at a few Halloween facts:

- More than 50 million Americans will celebrate Halloween this year.

- Of all adults, Americans in their twenties and thirties are the most likely to party this Halloween.

- Reusable decorations are increasingly popular. Decorations have extended to the outdoors, with Halloween yard signs, door decorations, and traditional ghosts, bats, witches, pumpkins, and vampires among the most popular items.

• Purple and green have emerged as accent colors to be used with old favorites orange and black.

There are a lot more interesting facts that we will look at more closely in Chapter 5, "Everybody's Doing It." However, the facts mentioned above give us a glimpse at the growth in popularity that Halloween has experienced in the last few years. Believe it or not, people are even building careers based on the demand for Halloween paraphernalia. Take for example Victor Moray of Washington. The .former dental laboratory technician has gone from making dentures to making fangs. "I used to make bridges and partials," says Moray, 25, "but I got bored with that job." Since 1992, working out of a store called "Gargoyle Statuary" (in the University District of Seattle), he has made thousands of fangs for Halloween party-goers, vampire enthusiasts, and more.[3]

Halloween has become one of the most widely celebrated festivals on the contemporary American calendar. It is not an official holiday, with no federal decree granting a day off from work, yet people just do it. Whether it's a parade in New York's Greenwich Village or a neighborhood costume party in the Midwest, Halloween is an American tradition that's here to stay.

There is a question that still remains to be answered: How will you as a parent or concerned adult respond to the tremendous influence of Halloween on our culture? More specifically, what will you do about Halloween and your family this year? There is cause for concern, but there are some creative ways to respond that will still be fun for your kids without compromising biblical values. We will explore these later in this book.

2

Costumes, Tricks, and Smiling Pumpkins

I grew up in the San Francisco Bay Area, in Northern California. I remember as a child looking forward to the adventure of dressing up in costumes and canvassing our neighborhood—with my brother and sister—to obtain as much candy and goodies as possible. My most vivid trick-or-treat memories are of living on Fairview Place, in Los Gatos.

We lived in a big old white house, with lots of big oak trees and a small creek running through our huge yard. Fairview Place was nestled in the foothills above the city and was comprised of about 15 houses and a couple of duplexes. Every Halloween my parents would help my brother, sister, and me come up with a costume. Sometimes we bought them and other times we would design our own. In either case, our costumes were mild by today's standards. None of the horror stuff for us. Instead, we dressed up as cowboys, athletes, pirates, animals, and ballerinas (for my sister). Because everything had to be "fair," my parents would give each of us the exact same bag to use for gathering goodies. Then my parents would bundle up and walk door-to-door with us as we yelled out "trick-or-treat!"

Ms. Wren's House

By the end of our journey around the neighborhood, our bags were full of all kinds of goodies that we would now have to carefully protect from a sibling who might be tempted to take something extra for himself or herself. However, the highlight of our trick-or-treat experience each year was finishing our evening adventure at old Ms. Wren's house. The narrow path leading to her front door was lit from the glow of the lights inside her small cottage.

She would answer the door, wearing one of her handmade aprons and displaying a broad smile on her face. Once inside, we warmed ourselves with hot cider or cocoa and enjoyed homemade caramel apples or popcorn balls with other kids from the neighborhood. While we ate, we shared highlights of the evening's adventure with Ms. Wren. If there was enough time, Ms. Wren would crank up her antique Victrola and we would all stand around listening to the funny-sounding music that the old records produced.

Were we celebrating Halloween? I hardly think so, but my family was having fun gathering goodies and spending time with other people from the neighborhood. Maybe you also remember having a similar Halloween experience growing up: having fun dressing up in costumes and canvassing your neighborhood to obtain as much candy and goodies as possible. But unfortunately, times and neighborhoods have changed.

Families move more frequently, people hardly know who their neighbors are, and there is a greater concern for personal safety. More and more people are looking for alternatives to participate in during Halloween. We will discuss the difference between celebrating Halloween and participating in alternatives in a subsequent chapter. But for now let's examine some of the traditional practices of Halloween and where they originated.

Trick-or-Treating

There are several ideas about where the custom of trick-or-treating began. Some have their roots in Ireland hundreds of years ago. The first practice involved a group of farmers who went from house to house begging food for the village new year festivities in the name of their ancient gods. Good luck was promised to all who donated, but threats were made against those who would not give.

The second practice began as a response to the action of evil spirits. Young people would build huge bonfires in the hills, and the bright glow would cause townspeople to put out sweets and goodies to entreat the evil spirits to pass them by. After the fires would burn down, the children would enter town and make off with the goodies. If they found no sweets, they would perform a prank on the villagers. Many superstitious townspeople believed that evil spirits would come into their houses and sour milk, kill their cattle, or poison their water wells.

Another tradition was that in early times people in scary disguise went around on Halloween night asking for alms. For the gifts received they would pray or fast for lost souls, who, it was believed, would gratefully give their goodwill to the donors. People who did not respond to the request would be haunted by the spirits of the neglected dead.

Trick-or-treating also seems to be related to the Gaelic practice of giving cakes to the poor at Samhain or "summer's-end," a seasonal festival that coincides with All Souls' Day. They came to be called "soul-cakes," and in return recipients were obligated to pray for a good harvest. Even closer is an English "Plough Day" custom. Ploughmen went about begging for gifts, and if they did not receive anything, they threatened damage to the grounds with their ploughs.

The Halloween begging activity of trick-or-treating is a more recent American phenomenon and dates back to the 1930s. It is a custom that was intended to control and displace communally disruptive pranking activities. Ironically, today it is viewed as a potentially dangerous activity and in some people's opinion is in need of institutional control.

Prior to the 1960s Halloween was widely seen as an opportunity for child's play and adolescent pranks. Today it can be a scary night for both parents and children, especially the practice of trick-or-treating. Reports of anonymous sadists who laced candy with poison or razor blades began to affect the practice of trick-or-treating as early as the 1970s. In the 1980s these fears were augmented by alarming news reports that satanic cults were kidnapping and murdering children.[4]

In 1990 it was reported that Ariel Katz, a young seven-year-old Santa Monica girl, collapsed while trick-or-treating. Local police believed she had eaten poisoned candy from her bag of goodies. The authorities conducted an intense door-to-door search in the girl's neighborhood, blocking off streets, confiscating candy, and interviewing residents. Later reports conceded that Katz had died of congenital heart failure, not poison or drugs. But the nationwide publicity of her case fueled panic fires of concern.[5]

More than 75 percent of all reported cases about booby-trapped candy or other outrageous allegations have involved no injury at all. Detailed follow-up reports have concluded that most accounts were hoaxes concocted by children or parents. New Halloween customs represent the

attempt by well-meaning adults to appropriate the holiday. However, there is nothing new about adults wishing to
"sanitize" Halloween. In the 1920s there was a nationwide
effort to solve the "Halloween problem." Civic and religious organizations in many communities argued that
good-natured pranks often associated with the season had
become too archaic. Youthful energy needed to be channeled into organized parties and charitable drives to collect food.[6]

Ironically, this early effort to "tame" Halloween also
brought forth the first widespread practice of trick-or-treating. Previous to this it was a custom found mostly among
Irish-based communities and was as likely to be attached
to Thanksgiving or Christmas as to Halloween. Thus you
could say it was adults who took the trick out of treating.

Costumes

The earliest origin of wearing costumes at Halloween
dates back to the time of the Druids. On the evening of
October 31, huge bonfires were built to offer animal, crop,
and sometimes human sacrifices to the sun god Muck Olla,
and to Samhain, the god of death. During this ritual the
people wore costumes made of animal heads and skins.
They danced, sang, and even jumped over the flames or
dashed through them. All of this was done to frighten evil
spirits away.

It was also the Druids' belief that on the eve of the
Celtic New Year (November 1), the god of death would call
together the wicked souls of those who had died within the
last 12 months. These "evil spirits" would then be sent to
attack people on the eve before the November 1 celebration. It was thought that the only way people could escape
was by assuming disguises so that they could not be recognized.

Considering the fact that trick-or-treating in the United States dates back only to the 1930s, it is hard to make too much of a direct connection between the Druid custom of wearing costumes and the current Halloween tradition. However, considering the fact that Halloween has evolved into the third-most-popular U. S. holiday party occasion for adults, and that an estimated 90 percent of all families with children 12 and younger will participate in trick-or-treating or a costume party, there is no denying the fact that costumes and Halloween go hand in hand.

With many businesses (including hospitals and banks) encouraging employees to "dress up" on Halloween, there is a huge market for costume sales among adults as well as kids. K-Mart offers a wide array of costumes in its "Scarewood Forest," while Target invites you to visit "Pumpkin Hollow." The Oriental Trading Company publishes a special catalog just for Halloween. Current costume selections include Star Wars characters, Mighty Morphin Power Rangers, Indian princesses, X-Men wolverines, Superman, Winnie the Pooh, M & M candy, Batman, Ninjas, Gorillas, Fairy princesses, Crusaders, clowns, the Crypt Keeper, Dilbert, Spiderman, and bumblebees.

Then there are the traditional offerings of the devil, ghosts, vampires, witches, grim reaper, skeletons, green monsters, and aliens. In the recent past adults have even had the opportunity to purchase a Princess Diana or O. J. Simpson costume. And don't forget all the necessary accessory items. There are crowns, hats, badges, wigs, masks, rubber hands, monster feet, fake teeth, and makeup.

Smiling Pumpkins

The jack-o'-lantern tradition grew out of Celtic belief during the Dark Ages. Jack-o'-lanterns were carved from turnips to ward off evil spirits. Legend has it that the jack-o'-lantern is the lantern of an Irish watchman who loved to play pranks on God and the devil. Because of this, he was cursed to carry his lantern throughout all time to light the way for the spirit world.

Another viewpoint on this practice says that the jack-o'-lantern is actually an ancient symbol for a "damned soul." It is said that the lanterns were actually named for a man called "Irish Jack." Legend has it that Jack was a stingy drunk who tricked the devil into climbing an apple tree for an apple. Jack then cut the sign of a cross into the trunk of the tree, thereby preventing the devil from coming down again. Then Jack forced the devil to swear he would never come after Jack's soul. The devil reluctantly agreed.

When Jack eventually died, he was turned away at the gates of heaven because of his problem with the bottle and his life of selfishness. After being sent to hell, the devil also rejected Jack, keeping his earlier promise. Since Jack could not enter either heaven or hell, he was condemned to wander the earth. As he was leaving hell, eating a turnip, the devil threw a hot coal at him. Jack put the coal in his turnip and was doomed to wander in darkness with his "jack-o'-lantern" until judgment day. With this tradition in mind, people began to hollow out turnips, placing candles inside to scare away evil spirits from their houses.

Much of the Halloween tradition, including the jack-o'-lantern, was brought to America by Irish immigrants. However, the turnip was replaced by the pumpkin in America.

Today pumpkin-carving contests require the participants to purchase a whole array of special carving tools to help create a Halloween masterpiece. You also find smiling pumpkins associated in numerous other ways with Halloween. For example, there are jack-o'-lantern candles, beanbag creatures, wooden pumpkin ring toss games, yard spinners, candy, hanging minilights, doorknob covers, wind socks, flashlights, and even a plastic stuff-a-pumpkin family.

A Personal Decision

We could fill many pages examining the various traditions and their origins that people have practiced at Halloween. Many adults have continued to carry out Halloween traditions of their childhood with their own kids. History has a way of repeating itself in many different forms. However, as you can see, the mainstream practice of Halloween traditions today is totally divorced from the macabre roots of early festivals.

Is it right for a Christian to continue practicing the previously mentioned Halloween traditions? If so, what is the appropriate way? If not, why not? It is a decision that all parents and concerned adults must make. Nevertheless, before you decide, let's examine some additional information together. Then you can make the best decision, one that you will feel comfortable with, and one that is best for your family.

Witches, Ghosts, and Things That Go Bump in the Night

Poltergeists, witches on broomsticks, ghosts, and bats seem to be everywhere at Halloween. From decorations to costumes to candy, they seem to go hand in hand with Halloween festivities. But aside from Halloween, what do we need to know about them and how should we respond? No discussion on Halloween would be complete without these things that "go bump in the night."

Ghosts and Spirits

A dominant theme of Halloween originating with the ancient Druids has been death, ghosts, and spirits. Aside from Halloween, ghost stories and spooks are everywhere today. Although Halloween comes and goes, interest in the spirit phenomena continues throughout the year.

Poltergeists, ghosts, and supernatural happenings have found their way into popular movies such as *Fallen* with Denzel Washington, *Ghost Dad* with Bill Cosby, *Ghost* with

Patrick Swayze, and *Ghost Busters*, which has also become a popular cartoon. Then there are dozens of TV specials and segments on programs, such as "Unsolved Mysteries," "The X Files," "Star Trek," "Sightings," "The Extraordinary," and "Paranormal Borderline," that captivate millions of viewers each week. Programmers do not leave the public lacking during the year for stories on poltergeists and ghosts. ("Poltergeist" comes from two German words that literally translated mean "noisy ghost.")

The theories to explain or identify poltergeists and ghosts are very diverse. The three most common explanations are: 1) the Christian view that poltergeists are biblical demons; 2) the parapsychological belief that poltergeists constitute an entirely human phenomenon as a result of various manifestations of alleged psychic power (i.e. psychokinetic); 3) the mediumistic interpretation that poltergeists are the roaming spirits of the human dead. Considered objectively, poltergeists and ghosts are very difficult to explain apart from the supernatural. The theories of human or natural origin are simply inadequate.

Poltergeists involve an awesome number of different manifestations and insidious incidents. These may include cold rooms, thick and oppressive air, terrible foul smells, unusual malignant voices, bizarre creature or humanlike apparitions, movement of objects (including some that are heavy), strange markings on people or furniture, spontaneous fires, electromagnetic occurrences, unusual physical symptoms, and so on.

Psychic researchers, parapsychologists, and occultists who investigate these phenomena seem to consider the demonic theory hardly worth mentioning. Nevertheless, the demonic theory is far more believable than the idea that human psychic energy can account for the kinds of occurrences that take place. And the poltergeist occurrences seem to support the same goals as those of evil spirits which the Bible identifies as demons.

Halloween has the potential of leading people to have a fascination with ghosts. If you have any doubts about involvement with these "demonic spirits" discussed above, keep in mind what God's Word teaches on this subject. In Paul's instructions to Timothy he writes, "The Spirit clearly says that in later times some will abandon the faith and follow deceiving spirits and things taught by demons" (1 Timothy 4:1). And in even stronger language Paul warns the believers at Corinth, "I do not want you to be participants with demons" (1 Corinthians 10:20).

Bats

Spooky Halloween storytelling often includes warty-nosed witches sprinkling bat wings into bubbling cauldrons. And of course Halloween decorating could hardly be complete without a few black bats.

Unfortunately, Halloween has given bats a bad name. For example, did you know that bats mostly eat insects? Some even eat fish, lizards, and frogs. Only a very few (one-third of 1 percent) drink blood. Most people do not realize that bats are not dirty creatures, but are really quite clean. Only a few bats ever contract rabies, and they seldom transmit it to people.

In fact bats are basically gentle animals. If you leave them alone, they will do the same to you. Most bats live in caves, and as many as 20 million or more might live in the same cave. They are the only flying mammals, and they have hair instead of feathers. Some are as small as bumblebees and weigh less than a penny, while others are so large that they measure six feet from wingtip to wingtip and weigh more than two pounds. Most people do not realize that some species of bats fly from flower to flower and pollinate plants so the flowers will produce seeds. Some even scatter seeds from which new plants grow.

Yet despite all the positive "bat facts," bats are in trouble today for a number of reasons. More than half of all American bat species are endangered or threatened. Most people have a fear of bats (Halloween doesn't help) and want to kill them. People don't understand the important role bats play in the balance of nature, so they disturb the bats' caves and cut down their forest homes. In some countries people eat bats, while in other places they poison them by accident when they spray their crops.

Halloween has no doubt helped to create some not-so-accurate "bat facts." But that doesn't mean you should become overly friendly with them, either. You should never handle a bat. Any bat you can catch is likely to be sick or injured. You may never become a "bat fan," but at least now we have cleared up some of the more common misconceptions about these important animals.

Witches

Witchcraft is one of the most common themes of Halloween. However, our society's image of witchcraft is changing from that of something evil to that of something supernaturally positive. Look at ABC's popular prime-time television show, "Sabrina, the Teenage Witch." Or how about a popular magazine for girls that says witchcraft is a cool religion? "Witchcraft Is a Religion" is the title of an article that appeared in an issue of *Sassy* Magazine, where several witches were interviewed, including a 16-year-old aspiring young actress.[7] Unfortunately, witchcraft is really not "cool" or a laughing matter.

For Laurie Cabot, the 60-year-old official witch of Salem, Massachusetts, and one of more than 9 million witches worldwide, witchcraft is an earth-based religion with heavy environmental overtones. According to the article in

Sassy, witches are not Satanists and don't believe in evil, Satan, or sacrificing animals. Doing evil is supposedly against one of the basic principles of their religion: If you do anything bad, it comes back to you three times. So any magic that witches do is "for the good of all," as they say at the end of spells, which are like prayers to them.

Witchcraft (or wicca) has been a legally recognized religion in the United States since 1985. It has eight major holidays that revolve around the changing of the seasons. On these days covens, which are groups of three to 13 witches, form magic circles where they perform rituals and read spells. Covens are supposed to be good because there is a power in speaking your convictions in front of a group of people. Also "cool," according to *Sassy* magazine, is the fact that witchcraft has always been a very woman-centered or feminist religion. Although witches believe in many goddesses and gods, they maintain that the universe was created by a goddess, because only women have the ability to create life by giving birth. Most witches are women, although today more men are becoming interested in witchcraft.

Magic is a very important part of witchcraft. Any witch has the power to make things happen. According to Laurie Cabot, in her book *Power of the Witch: The Earth, the Moon, and the Magical Path to Enlightenment,* magic is performed in an altered state of consciousness called alpha, in which fewer brainwaves register per second. She gives step-by-step instructions for going into alpha by counting back from the number 7 and relaxing. Apparently witches can use this altered state to do all of their magic, from things as simple as getting a parking place to work as serious as cleaning up the environment or performing psychic healings. Cabot's book goes on to describe how anyone can learn to do these things, as well as how spells are written, how words are used to conduct energy, and how magic potions are made.

Cats are important to witches because they are their connection to the animal world (they call them "familiars"). Witches also use crystals and wear pentacles (a pentacle is a five-pointed star inside a circle that is said to bring wisdom and protection). All witches wear black for rituals because it contains all the colors of the rainbow.

Searching People

Many of the people who study witchcraft are searching for spiritual truth and the supernatural. Kaytee, a 16-year-old high school junior who wants to be an actress, is a witch. So is her mother, her father, and her eight-year-old sister. Kaytee's parents are first-degree witches, but she is still practicing for initiation. She is learning the basics of alpha and about the gods and goddesses of the magic circle. Everyone at her school knows she is into witchcraft, although most of her peers don't understand it.[8] Kaytee says she is going to use her first spell to help her get the part of Peter Pan in the school play. "It's like prayer," she says. "I will project that I will get this part of Peter Pan in the musical, harm me none and for the good of all."

Even though for some people the feminist and environmental aspects of witchcraft are enticing, the big draw is power. According to Laurie Cabot, "Witchcraft is a connectedness to everything, so you can center yourself and feel as if you can control some of your environment a little more. I think teenagers today need their own power. They need to feel that they can help shape the future."[9]

As you can tell, the "Old Religion" (dating back to early paganism) of witchcraft is experiencing renewed interest today, especially among teenagers. Unfortunately, witchcraft is not "cool" or a laughing matter. Let's look at what the Bible has to say about it.

The Witchcraft Warnings

Witchcraft can be defined as the performance of magic forbidden by God for nonbiblical purposes. The word "witchcraft" is related to the old English word "wiccan," the "practice of magical arts." Both the Old and New Testaments make repeated references to the practice of witchcraft and sorcery. In every instance where these practices are mentioned, they are condemned by God. The Bible forbids all forms of witchcraft, including sorcery, astrology, and magic.

God is so concerned about this subject that He very specifically warns us in His Word to stay away from it. In 2 Chronicles we read about a man named Manasseh who became a king at the ripe old age of 12. But he did evil in the eyes of the Lord and paid a price for his bad choices. Here is what God said about Manasseh's involvement in witchcraft: "He [Manasseh] sacrificed his sons in the fire in the valley of Ben Hinnom, practiced sorcery, divination and witchcraft, and consulted mediums and spiritists. He did much evil in the eyes of the Lord, provoking him to anger" (2 Chronicles 33:6).

Just because this story is about a king who lived a couple of thousand years ago doesn't mean that God has changed His mind about practicing witchcraft today. This warning is just as relevant to us as it was in previous generations. Provoking God to anger is not a very smart thing to do. Why would God get angry about this kind of practice? Because He wants us to rely on *Him* for guidance, power, and direction. *He* is our strength and our life—not the forces of darkness.

In the book of Galatians the apostle Paul warns Christians to beware of the strong pull of the flesh that can cause us to fall into sin:

The acts of the sinful nature [flesh] are obvious: sexual immorality, impurity and debauchery [shamelessness]; idolatry and witchcraft; hatred, discord, jealousy, fits of rage, selfish ambition, dissensions, factions and envy; drunkenness, orgies, and the like. I warn you, as I did before, that those who live like this will not inherit the kingdom of God (Galatians 5:19-21).

What an ugly list of sins witchcraft has been included in! The word used here for witchcraft is translated from a Greek word (the original language of the New Testament) meaning drugs. In ancient times the worship of evil powers was accompanied by the use of drugs to create trances. Sound familiar? Drugs, witchcraft, and Satanism are still closely associated today. Drugs and alcohol are also a gateway for some people into the world of the occult.

The Forms of Witchcraft

As Christians we need to be prepared to respond to the influence of witchcraft that we encounter in our daily lives. Things associated with witchcraft can show up in a variety of ways and in many different places. Beware of the movies you go to see. Not all movies are bad, but some can entertain you in a subtle way with the principles of witchcraft. Take for example *Hocus Pocus*, starring Bette Midler, Sarah Jessica Parker, and Kathy Najimy. The plot portrays the three as long-dead seventeenth-century witches who are brought back to life one Halloween to suck the life out of children.[10]

It's silly, scary, and magical all at the same time, but it also can confuse you as to the response that God would want you to have toward witchcraft. When the film was first released, it was interesting to watch a number of witches come out against it in public interviews because the movie portrayed them in a negative light. I guess the truth hurts.

Satan has a way of entertaining us through a variety of forms of witchcraft as he makes it both fashionable and appealing. Take for example the rock band Fleetwood Mac. The female lead singer, Stevie Nicks, is a self-avowed white witch.[11] Yet she and the band performed in a reunion concert at one of the parties celebrating the inauguration of President Bill Clinton.

More Evil Than It Seems

When a witch is performing at that level it can be deceptive by making you think witchcraft can't be all that evil. Once again we can let down our guard by subjecting our minds to the music of many popular bands on the scene today. And it's not just rock music either; the usually subtle messages can be found in any number of contemporary styles.

Witchcraft and its subtle influences can also be found in games for your PC, Nintendo, fantasy role-playing games, board games, and even comic books. It is not practical in a book like this to attempt to name every movie, video, television show, game, or band that may make use of magic spells, incantations, or any other form of witchcraft. Things change so rapidly in the entertainment scene that it's impossible to keep track of everything that happens. The point is to stay alert to the subtle influences of witchcraft in your entertainment.

Another popular avenue for witchcraft today is the environmental movement. There has never been a generation so environmentally conscious as the generation of today. And witches are at the forefront of encouraging us to "be nice to Mother Earth." While we certainly need to do our part in being environmentally sensitive, we need to be careful not to get things out of balance.

As Christians, God has called us to be caretakers of the planet. In Genesis 2:15 we read, "The LORD God took the man and put him in the Garden of Eden to work it and take care of it. " But the Bible also teaches us to worship the Creator, not the creation. In Exodus 20:3 God says, "You shall have no other gods before me." Don't be deceived: While witchcraft may appear to be cool and helping the environment, it goes about it in all the wrong ways. We must always keep our eyes and hearts centered on God as we strive to do the right thing.

What happens if a good friend or a child starts to show an interest in magic spells or some other form of witchcraft? How should we respond? We should start by asking God to help us find out why this person is interested in magic spells or incantations. Sometimes people start playing around with this stuff at parties out of curiosity. They want to see if there is really any power that can be gained. Dabbling like this can be dangerous because it can be a gateway to the occult for some people.

For others, a fascination with magic spells or other forms of witchcraft can be a sincere search for power to change their lives or deal with the pain of a broken home, rejection, or hopelessness. Witchcraft may appear to offer immediate power for change, but it is at best temporary. It also causes us to leave God out of the picture and to rely on evil powers instead.

God wants to use us in the lives of our friends and family members, to help them realize that the power we all need to handle the pressures of life is found in the resurrection of Jesus Christ. This same power that God used to bring Jesus back to life after being in the grave for three days is available to us to help us overcome all the challenges in our daily life.

The Power of Prayer

The best way to apply this power is through prayer. When you or someone you care about is facing tough times, ask God for His strength and wisdom to face the situation. Put your energy and effort into prayerfully seeking God's help and answers. Also make sure you are getting a steady diet of "spiritual food" from God's Word. The Bible is God's handbook for living and it contains supernatural guidance that only God can give. Remember, there is no substitute for time alone studying the Bible. Don't fall into the trap of quick "microwavable" answers seemingly gained from chants and spells; go to the Author of life itself and trust God.

Satan will do anything he can to candy-coat evil to make it easier to seduce us away from our family, our church, and our God. Don't be confused by Laurie Cabot and other witches who sprinkle bits of truth in their concern about the environment, equal treatment of the sexes, and other problems that plague our society. We all need to do our part in making positive changes in society, but we also need to take our direction from the absolute truth of God's Word and let Him help us solve the difficult issues of life.

PART TWO

What in the World Is Going On?

4

Evil Goes Mainstream

In the last few years there has been a tremendous rise in the preoccupation with evil and the occult throughout the world. People of all ages are fascinated with things that are evil. They are easily tempted to dabble to see what will happen if they do some wicked thing. It's almost as if people are trying to see how close they can get to the fire without getting burned. And for some people Halloween is a good excuse to experiment.

Some people are enticed to play with evil because they're interested in forces and power greater than they are—the secret, mysterious world of the fourth dimension or the supernatural. In other cases people are looking for help to deal with the difficult issues of life. But evil can also be interesting and appealing to someone who is bored, without meaning and purpose in life.

If you get up every day and go through the same routine with no goals or aspirations, wickedness and the things of the occult can look pretty exciting. Your curiosity is piqued, you get interested, and the fascination with evil begins. This fascination quickly turns into a growing appetite, and potentially an obsession with the forces of darkness. Most of the time things evolve so gradually that you don't even realize what you're getting into. Slowly and subtly you get sucked in, unaware of what has been happening. No one ever wakes up one morning and suddenly decides to go out and become a psychopath.

But let's face it—one of the most appealing ways that evil can appear to be innocent is when it's portrayed as being fun and entertaining, such as at Halloween. Movies, cartoons, costumes, books, music, and games can sometimes have an element of wickedness that seems to "bait and hook" your interest.

And there's no doubt that this kind of evil sells. Take *Sin* magazine, for example. Here's a publication designed for kids who are "skaters" and "thrashers" that is supposed to communicate the latest in art, music, culture, and "the Scene." All this is done with occultic artwork and articles encouraging rebellion, immoral sex, and voodoo comics. Or consider how megaselling author Stephen King's novels come to life in theaters, thereby desensitizing millions of people to vile wickedness. And what about the latest in skateboard designs? They are made to look as evil as possible, according to a national champion, because "kids are into evil." When evil comes packaged in the form of entertainment or recreation, it disarms us to its dangers and to the truth that we are playing with spiritual fire. And playing with fire can get you burned!

The Origin of Evil

Have you ever wondered how you know when something is evil, and where evil came from? Webster's dictionary defines evil as "that which is wicked, arising from bad character and causing discomfort or harm." In general the Bible defines evil as being bad and harmful: bad in the sense that doing something evil is disobeying God, and *harmful* in the consequences received as a result of disobedience. To do evil is to be in opposition toward God, which ultimately is sin.

The origin of evil came out of the freedom of choice exercised in the angelic realm. Evil was a necessary risk when God, in creation, allowed each person and each angelic being to have a free will. God knew there was the possibility of someone choosing to go his own way and to rebel against Him. And that is exactly what Lucifer (Satan) did. In Ezekiel 28:15 we read that "wickedness was found in you." There is no definitive explanation given as to what caused Satan to choose evil, but the effects of his choice are still with us today.

We don't know the complete reason why God allows evil, but we do know that He is able to bring glory to Himself through the presence of evil by expressing the grace and justice that are part of His character. Paul explains it this way in Romans 9:22,23: "What if God, choosing to show his wrath and make his power known, bore with great patience the objects of his wrath—prepared for destruction? What if he did this to make the riches of his glory known to the objects of his mercy, whom he prepared in advance for glory?" By allowing evil and wickedness in our world, God can also demonstrate the awesome forgiveness, love, and care that He has for each one of us.

The Bible teaches that the one behind all of the wickedness in the world is Satan himself, the "granddaddy of evil." In 2 Thessalonians 3:3 he is called the "evil one." Satan is evil, and sometimes his evil can even appear to be beautiful. The devil began his wicked work back at the beginning of human history with the first man and woman—Adam and Eve—and has not changed his tactics since then (see Genesis 3).

The Disease of Sin

Because of Adam and Eve's choice to disobey God, you and I inherited this spiritual disease called sin. The Bible describes sin as rebellion against God (Joshua 1:17,18), knowing the right thing to do and not doing it (James 4:17), and missing the mark or standard that God has set before us (Romans 3:23).

And though this evil spiritual disease is worse than cancer and AIDS because it has the potential to claim everyone's life *spiritually*, there is a remedy for it. Romans 5:8 says, "But God demonstrates his own love for us in this: While we were still sinners, Christ died for us." The antidote for sin is found in a personal relationship with God through His Son, Jesus.

The confusing world system in which we live would like us to believe that there is no such thing as sin or evil, and that everything is relative: What is right for us can be determined by our own belief system, and someone else can believe the exact opposite and also be right. This concept of relative truth is one of the key elements of the New Age movement.

The devil's evil influence can be seen in many different forms in the world in which we live. This evil influence shapes the things that can tempt us to rebel against God. Pick up a newspaper or watch the evening news on CNN and you can see the effects of wickedness in the world. Broken families, terrorism, racial tension, murder, rape, suicide, and abuse are just a few of consequences of evil and trying to live independent of God.

Every day we are involved in a conflict with the world. This conflict has the potential to lure us into a hostile disobedience toward God. In l John 2:15 we are warned not to love the things of the world. The world in this case is the organized system headed by Satan which leaves God out and is a rival to Him. The values and the attitudes that characterize this system are the lust of the flesh, the lust of the eyes, and the boastful pride of life (see l John 2:16).

These things are of the world and they won't last. We are told not to love these things because they are not from God. And if the weaknesses of our human flesh are left unchecked, patterns can develop that can be deadly to our spiritual well-being. By contrast, God values self-control, a spirit of generosity, and humble service. When Satan attacks you with his temptations, focus in on true contentment and where it comes from. Learn not only to say no, but also to be satisfied with who you are and what you have. The key is to trust God and to depend upon Him for direction in every dimension of your life.

If we are to respond to God in the way He desires and to live the quality of life He has designed for us, then we must stop acting on motives that reflect the world's value system. We need to be thankful and satisfied with what God has provided for us in our lives.

Make sure to check the heavenly loyalty of your heart and the focus of your mind. As you do this, remember to follow the advice of the psalmist to "turn from evil and do good" (Psalm 34:14).

Satan is up to no good and will do everything in his power to defeat God's will for your life. And he doesn't always approach everyone in the same way. What is temptation for one person may or may not be a problem for someone else. For a guy named Mark David Chapman, the search for power became an opening for Satan's evil influence in his life. And it had disastrous results.

The Search for Power

It was the early '60s, when the Beatles' popularity had exploded in America. Mark David Chapman's family lived in Decatur, Georgia, where his father gave Mark his first rock 'n' roll album, "Meet the Beatles." Like millions of fans in America, nine-year-old Mark immediately fell under the spell of Beatlemania and would be influenced dramatically by the Beatles' music, even as an adult.

Mark was also a very lonely child who would often escape into a world of imaginary people. According to Chapman, he had hundreds of thousands of them living in the walls of his bedroom, and he was their king. It was the only way he could cope with an abusive father. His dad would strike his mother, and sometimes in the middle of the night Mark would run into their room and try to break up the fight. At other times he himself was abused as his father would strike him with a belt.

When Mark was 14, the Beatles released "Magical Mystery Tour," an album filled with drug-inspired imagery. Mark eagerly entered into the world of LSD. Several years later Mark thought he had found direction for his life working with refugees as a YMCA camp counselor. Everyone thought he was terrific, including his staff of 15.

Then the camp closed down and he decided to go to college. He went from being a "big man at camp" to a nobody on campus—the same kind of nobody he was when he was a little kid. Severe depression then took over Mark's life. He dropped out of college and bought a one-way ticket to Hawaii to kill himself.

After buying a cheap piece of plastic vacuum cleaner hose at Sears, he found a seemingly deserted spot on the north shore of the island. He hooked up the hose to the exhaust of a car and sat in the car after turning the engine on. But he was discovered by some people and rescued from his attempted suicide.

After a few weeks in the hospital he was released, got a job, and met a travel agent named Gloria. He and Gloria fell in love and were married. The honeymoon was quickly over as Gloria watched this quiet, gentle man turn into a violent, unpredictable stranger. When Mark got frustrated he would grab his wife and hit her, just as his father had done with Mark's mother.

Mark seemed to be struggling to find himself. He drifted from job to job and was moody and unpredictable. Deep down inside he was losing his grip on reality. At the same time he seemed to become obsessed with a book titled *Catcher in the Rye*, the story of a teenager who left school on a three-day journey to find himself. After looking in various places in Manhattan, the main character of the book didn't find anything but a bunch of phoniness.

So Chapman assumed the identity of the fictional teenager from the book and became a believer in the character's campaign against phoniness. One day while visiting his once-peaceful oasis, the public library, Mark came across a book about Beatle John Lennon called *One Day at a Time*. As he looked at the pictures he began judging Lennon, especially after learning that Lennon lived in a very expensive and exclusive co-op called "The Dakota" in Manhattan. This angered Chapman because he thought Lennon had sold out on the Beatles' earlier idealism. Their idealism had meant a lot to Mark, but now he felt Lennon had betrayed it and so he became enraged.

In Mark David Chapman's disturbed mind the pieces were falling into place. He was caught in an unstoppable spiral down. There was a great despair and emptiness of feeling, as if he were a king-sized nobody. But at the same time he saw this real somebody who he perceived to be a "big-time phony." Suddenly this "nobody" was wanting to strike down this "somebody."

Mark bought a pistol and a plane ticket to New York City. When he checked out of his maintenance-man job for the last time, he signed out as "John Lennon." He went to New York's Central Park to prepare to eliminate this phony "somebody." In a television interview later, Chapman said that before he killed Lennon he turned to Satan, because he knew he wouldn't have the strength to kill a man on his own.[12] So he went through what he thought was an appropriate satanic ritual: He took off all his clothes and chanted and screamed and howled. "I asked Satan to give me the power to kill John Lennon," Chapman said.[13] Mark David Chapman shot and killed John Lennon in front of "The Dakota" apartments. He was sentenced to 20 years to life in prison.

Mark David Chapman went searching for power to help him accomplish something that would give him a sense of significance, and he claims he found it in Satan. In some ways Mark is no different from a lot of people today who are looking for a source of power to help them deal with the pain of life or to change their circumstances. Yet he took his search to the extreme, and his life was filled with warning signs that he would be susceptible to the occult.

His abusive family situation, his drug use, and his extreme loneliness should have been an indication that something was desperately wrong in his life. But more obvious than anything else was his lack of identity. In his desire to escape the pain of life and find security, acceptance, and significance, Mark lost his grip on reality. He had already given Satan a number of areas to establish footholds in his life, so he was set up to fall when Satan tempted him with power.

The Intrigue of Evil

Power is an interesting concept and is often part of the intrigue of evil. It can create havoc and corruption if it is obtained from the wrong source and abused, as it was with Chapman. It is alluring because it is a means of control, authority, or influence over others. I have talked with a number of people who say the power they have gotten from Satan has made them feel special. It gives them a sense of significance among their peers.

Before you write off Mark Chapman as just another crazy guy, concluding that no one else could ever be drawn down that same road, remember that our enemy possesses supernatural power and abilities. The more footholds you give the devil in your life, the easier it becomes to subtly slip away from God and into evil. Remember, if Satan can get you to *believe* a lie he can get you to *live* one as well. Mark didn't wake up one day and all of a sudden decide to murder John Lennon; it happened subtly. The words that a gang member from Los Angeles painted on the side of a building could just as easily have been Chapman's: "Ashes to ashes, dust to dust, if God won't help me then Satan must."

The Bible speaks much about power. The power of Jesus Christ is described as supreme (Ephesians 1:20,21), unlimited (Matthew 28:18), everlasting (l Timothy 6:16), and able to subdue all things (Philippians 3:21). It was demonstrated when Jesus rose from the dead (John 2:19), thus overcoming the world (John 16:33) and Satan (Colossians 2:15) and destroying the works of Satan (l John 3:8).

Satan's evil power is a counterfeit—limited and temporary—designed to lure people away from trusting God. Our source of *real* power comes only from God; only He "gives strength to the weary and increases the power of the weak. Even youths grow tired and weary, and young men stumble and fall; but those who hope in the LORD will renew their strength. They will soar on wings like eagles; they will run and not grow weary, they will walk and not be faint" (Isaiah 40:29-31). The key to obtaining this power is to put your hope in God and not in the things of this world. The same power that raised Jesus from the grave is available to you to help you face the challenges of life. Access to this power is granted when you receive Jesus Christ as your Savior and Lord.

We live in an evil and seductive world. However, God has given us all the resources we need through His Son, His Spirit, prayer, and the Bible to help us avoid every form of evil in our lives. "For God did not give us a spirit of timidity, but a spirit of power, of love and of self-discipline" (2 Timothy 1:7). When we are bored or tempted, or need help and power to overcome the difficulties of life, we need to turn to Christ. He should be our first resource, not our last resort.

Mainstream Halloween celebrations may be part of evil's manifestation in our society, but they are not what God wants to influence our lives. So don't be fascinated with evil. Instead start getting absorbed with God!

5

Everybody's Doing It

Each year around Halloween time we receive many requests for interviews on national radio and television shows. This is due in part to our first two book projects: *The Seduction of Our Children* and *The Devil's Playground*. I never cease to be amazed at the questions and comments that come from the mouths of some people. For example, there was Phil, who lives in Toronto. That day I was a guest on the "Lifeline" program hosted by my buddy Neil Boron on WDCX in Buffalo, New York.

Phil reminded Neil and me that as Christians we were to be "in the world, not of the world." He was also convinced that "if we just ignored the Halloween holiday, it would eventually go away and disappear." Unfortunately, that same mindset about Halloween (and other issues) is all too prevalent among well-meaning believers today. However, being a Christian ostrich and "burying your head in the sand" is not going to make Halloween or any other contemporary cultural issue vanish. The truth is that Halloween is here to stay. Instead of ignoring it, let's take a look at how popular it really is and then examine in a later portion of this book various ways in which we can respond to it.

Bigger Than You Think

Halloween has been known in North America since Colonial Days. By the middle of the twentieth century it was largely seen as a children's holiday. However, in the last few years it has exploded and has become one of the most widely celebrated festivals on the contemporary American calendar, even though it is not an official holiday. Take a look at these trends and facts.

- More than 50 million Americans celebrate Halloween each year.

- Halloween is second only to Christmas for holiday decorating. An estimated 50 percent of all Americans decorate for Halloween. (Eighty percent decorate for Christmas.) Purple and green have emerged as accent colors to be used with the traditional Halloween colors of orange and black.

- An estimated 90 percent of all families with children ages 12 and younger will participate in trick-or-treating or costume parties.

- Long popular with children, Halloween has evolved into the third-most-popular holiday party occasion for adults. (Christmas and New Year's Eve are first and second.) Approximately one-third of all adults will either host or attend a Halloween party. Of all adults, Americans in their twenties and thirties are the most likely to party this Halloween.

- Halloween workplace celebrations are on the rise. Many businesses allow employees to wear costumes for the day.

- Today's Halloween parties tend to be more sophisticated than those of five years ago. Research indicates that nearly half of all party planners spend several hours preparing, including shopping, cooking, and getting the house ready.

- Outdoor decorations are a big trend. Items like Halloween flags, door decorations, wind socks, and mobiles are especially popular today.[14]

- An estimated 400 million dollars is spent on Halloween each year. The lion's share is spent on candy and costumes. About 60 million dollars is earmarked for decorating and entertaining.

- Halloween is the eighth-largest seasonal card-sending occasion in the United States. An estimated 35 million Halloween cards will be exchanged this year, an increase of over 3 million from last year.[15]

A Piece of the Action

It seems like everyone wants a piece of the action when it comes to Halloween. Retailing giants like K-Mart welcome shoppers to "Scarewood Forest," while Target shoppers purchase their Halloween goodies at "Pumpkin Hollow." Goodyear Auto Service centers advertise Halloween specials. The Wichita, Kansas, Area Association of Realtors published a special newspaper insert in the *Wichita Eagle*, with suggested tips for keeping your home and property safe from vandals on Halloween.

Fast food outlet Taco Bell partnered with Universal Studios Hollywood to present Universal's "Halloween Horror Nights" at the Southern California theme park this year. The ten-dollar-off admission coupon advertised the 12 nights of horror this way: "Experience Halloween scares and thrills like never before. Run from aliens in Area 51. Come face-to-face with mutant sea creatures, meet every slasher known to mankind in the Crypt keeper's vault, nightly guillotine executions, the Circus of Freak, over 100 grotesque ghouls roaming about freely, plus so much gore! Halloween Horror Nights—live the Nightmare."

Other amusement parks across the country are also trying to "scare up" fall business. Roller coaster mecca Cedar Point in Sandusky, Ohio, launched its first Halloween festival in 1997, peppering the park with temporary haunted houses and other attractions. The theme park, which normally closes in September, lengthened its season by three weeks for the festival. Sesame Place in Langhorne, Pennsylvania, also started a Halloween fest in 1997 aimed at boosting attendance during a traditionally slow season. Six Flags' eight U.S. parks began adding October Halloween events in 1992, and Disney World (near Orlando) in 1995. Knott's Berry Farm, in Buena Park, California, added four new mazes and three new shows for its twenty-fifth annual Halloween Haunt in 1997.[16]

The Oriental Trading Company, based in Omaha, Nebraska, publishes an entire Halloween merchandise catalog. There are 80 pages packed with specialty items for the holiday. There are vinyl smile face vampire characters, glow-in-the-dark tracing figures, pumpkin tray tic-tac-toe, candles, games, removable tattoos, costumes, masks, soft vinyl body parts, wind-up chomping teeth, and slime cans with glow-in-the-dark eyeballs. There are even plastic light-up decorations, inflatable skeletons, and six-foot stuff-a-monsters available for your yard. And there are three easy ways to order these products!

New and Exciting?

New Halloween treats seem to appear each year to help add to the fiendish fun of the holiday. Here are some of the more recent offerings:

- Witch's capes. These capes are handmade by Lady Armida Barth, a wiccan high priestess and owner of the occult store "Lady in the Moon" in Manhattan's East Village. The capes come in a variety of styles and materials, although all are full-length and hooded. A velvet kid's version goes for 35 dollars, adults' satin, 45 dollars, and wool-lined with satin, 250 dollars.

- Spells. In Titania Hardie's new book, *Bewitched*, the third-generation white witch teaches the basics of spell-casting. This contemporary witch recommends incense and herbs in place of potions and eye-of-newt when casting spells.

- Masks. The New Orleans Mask Master has been making masks for more than 13 years. He offers hundreds of selections out of his store, "Masquerade Fantasy." His handcrafted leather masks will transform you into a clown, a devil, a crescent moon, or any of a dozen more images.

- Wine. Direct from Tarnave, a hilly region of Transylvania, comes Vampire Varietals, imported by Tri-Vin imports of Mount Vernon, New York. The merlot, cabernet, sauvignon blanc, and pinot griglo Vampire Varietals come complete with appropriate spooky labels. [17]

The TV networks pull out all the stops for Halloween-themed shows during the week leading up to October 31. The makers of "Hey Arnold!," the Nickelodeon cartoon, helped fans get into the Halloween spirit with a special "spooky" adventure created exclusively for *TV Guide*. The cartoon series also aired a new Halloween episode. "Goosebumps," on the Fox Network, featured a chilling two-part episode, "One Day at Horrorland." To appeal to kids and adults, the tried-and-true Simpsons aired another "Treehouse of Horror" episode.

A lot of the holiday fare skews to comedy. On ABC's "Home Improvement," the "Night to Dismember" episode has Mark featuring the family in his Halloween horror movie, and Tim using his "Tool Time" skills to build a hot rod jack-o'-lantern for a pumpkin-mobile race. Meanwhile, NBC's "Frasier" features a literary-themed costume ball. "Third Rock from the Sun" allows Dick to parade as a pirate, and Tommy and Sally to dress as Sonny and Cher.

Halloween parties also figure into the story lines of CBS's "The Gregory Hines Show," Fox's "Beverly Hills 90210," and ABC's "The Practice," "Nothing Sacred," "Sabrina, the Teenage Witch," and "Teen Angel." Halloween party themes were also featured in daytime dramas "Port Charles," "All My Children," "One Life to Live," and "General Hospital." Further, "Sabrina, the Teenage Witch" even pops up in "Boy Meets World." CBS's "Meego," "Cybill," and "George & Leo"; NBC's "Union Square"; Fox's "Living Single" and "Between Brothers"; and WB's "Unhappily Ever After," "The Jamie Foxx Show," and of course "Buffy the Vampire Slayer" also get into the spirit.

On the more serious side, the Learning Channel features a full week of prime-time ghouls. "Castle Ghosts of Wales" scares up the freakiest spooks supposedly haunting Welsh castles, with similar sightings later in the week regarding Ireland and Scotland. Actor Mark Hamill narrates "Mythical Beasts and Monsters," which separates history from lore. A&E's "Biography" profiles Boris Karloff, Lifetime's "Intimate Portrait" features witches, and the History Channel's "In Search of History" tracks Frankenstein. Last, but not least, American Movie Classics (AMC) scares up 26 films plus a "Monster Mania" documentary on fright movies. The one-hour show is hosted by onetime Dracula Jack Palace.

Expressing Identity

Besides being a highly commercialized "unofficial" holiday, Halloween is also used in a variety of ways by different groups of people as a vehicle for expressing identity. A university feminist group sponsors a ritual gathering, a mainline Protestant church sponsors a costume party for children, and a local charismatic church publicly denounces Halloween because it celebrates the devil, demons, and witchcraft. Some contemporary witches and pagans say Halloween is a holy day for them—one of the most sacred of the year. Halloween parades and street festivals have grown in popularity over the years in places like Georgetown (District of Columbia), San Francisco, and New York's Greenwich Village.

The neopagan ritual held outdoors is radically different from a church-sponsored harvest festival offered as an alternative. In each case, personal and group identity are being expressed through the medium of the holiday. What one does on or around Halloween depends on such factors as age, place of residence (rural, urban, suburban), region of the country, ethnicity, and peer group association. In certain parts of the country some communities have banned traditional Halloween celebrations altogether, replacing them with "harvest festivals" or "pumpkin fun days." And even though there is no federal decree or day given off for this "unofficial holiday," large numbers of people—kids and adults alike—still look for ways to express their personal opinion about Halloween.

It's Here to Stay

Contrary to Phil's advice at the beginning of this chapter, ignoring Halloween is not going to make it go away. How and why has it become so popular? Some would say it is due to the growing fascination with the occult in our culture. Others say it's because more adults today are looking for an excuse to dress silly, be with friends, and go to parties. Maybe it's because little kids know this is the one day of the year they can dress up in a fun costume and collect six month's worth of candy! Based on what we have examined, Halloween is not only here to stay, but in all probability it will continue to grow in popularity.

As Christians, we should not ignore what is going on around us in our culture. According to 2 Corinthians 5:20 we are called to be Christ's ambassadors. Jesus said that we are "the light of the world" and are to be influencers for the kingdom of God. "You are the salt of the earth. But if the salt loses its saltiness, how can it be made salty again? It is no longer good for anything, except to be thrown out and trampled by men" (Matthew 5:13).

If a seasoning has no flavor, it has no value. If Christians make no effort to have an effect on the world around them, they are of little value to God. If we act too much like the world, we are worthless. As Christians, we should not blend in with everybody else. Instead, we should affect them positively, just as seasoning brings out the best flavor in food.

When it comes to Halloween, somehow we must strive to achieve a balance between "conforming to the pattern of this world" that the apostle Paul warns against in Romans 12:2 and trying to ignore it in hopes that it will just vanish. Just because a lot of people are celebrating Halloween certainly doesn't mean that we should too. However, if we are to be salt and light in this world, the more fundamental issue for us as Christians is "What would Jesus do?" In Part Three we will examine various options a Christian can use to respond to this hugely popular celebration in our culture.

6

Satan Surfs
the Internet

The devil is everywhere today. Don't get the wrong idea; that's not a paranoid or fearful statement—just reality. Whether you are shopping in a mall at Halloween time, reading a street poster for a concert, or surfing the Internet, Satan's influence and image can be found. Halloween is said to be a special day on the calendar for Satan worshipers. Crimes related to the occult are on the rise. Yet there are many people, even in the church, who question the reality of his existence. And in the light of spiritual warfare, that's just the way the devil would like to keep it.

The spiritual battle we are all involved in is one of tremendous importance; it is a battle for our very souls. It is a war between the kingdom of light and the kingdom of darkness, between the kingdom of right and the kingdom of wrong, between the kingdom of God and the kingdom of Satan.

For us to fully understand the implications of this spiritual warfare we are engaged in, we must first understand the strategy and tactics of our enemy.

The Reality of Satan

The devil has done a masterful job at confusing us about his true identity. Plenty of movies, books, games, song lyrics, and celebrities represent Satan as something other than what he truly is. It's very easy to get the wrong idea about Satan and in the process lose sight of the intensity of the spiritual battle.

Most often we see Satan portrayed in one of two ways in the world. Sometimes he is pictured as a goofy little buffoon, wearing a red suit with horns on top of his head and carrying a strange-looking pitchfork with which he runs around poking people. I see this every Halloween in our neighborhood. Little kids go around trick-or-treating, dressed up as the devil in red polyester suits, carrying a plastic pitchfork. Yet they have no clue who they are imitating.

Satan is also portrayed in the opposite way: as a horrible-looking creature that is part human, part monster, and part alien; he has bulging evil eyes and fiery breath, and he possesses the most hideously wicked laugh imaginable. Stephen King novels and slasher movies are filled with these images. Even CD covers and comic books depict this kind of image of the devil. Satan has used these and other entertainment pictures of himself to confuse us and disarm us. If this is the only input that people in general get about the enemy, no wonder so many people today don't take him seriously! Unfortunately, Satan's strategy is working all too well.

In a national survey[18] the question was asked, "Is the devil for real?" Of those who responded, 47 percent who are associated with evangelical churches and 65 percent of mainline Protestants said no; Satan is merely a symbol of evil. Satan would like nothing better than for people, even those who claim to be Christians, to be deceived into believing that he doesn't actually exist. After all, if Satan isn't for real, then we don't have to be concerned about being on the alert and being prepared for spiritual warfare.

That's why it's critical to depend on what the Bible teaches regarding the devil. The world will give us confusing information when it comes to spiritual things. However, God's Word is the ultimate source for truth regarding every dimension of life. The Bible confirms the reality of the spiritual battle and gives us an accurate picture of the devil's true character.

In Ezekiel 28 we learn much about the true identity of Satan: "You were the model of perfection, full of wisdom and perfect in beauty.... You were blameless in your ways from the day you were created till wickedness was found in you.... Your heart became proud on account of your beauty, and you corrupted your wisdom because of your splendor. So I threw you to the earth; I made a spectacle of you before kings" (verses 12,15,17).

Satan was the wisest and most beautiful creature ever created, but he can only go as far and do as much as God allows. He is not an independent, equal rival of God. However, the devil does possess superhuman power and wisdom. Nothing else in all creation could compare to him. Still, despite the fact that Satan was given the most privileged position of any created being, he made a horrible choice to rebel against God. Ultimately the devil plunged all of creation into a deadly spiritual war.

It was Satan's incredible pride that led him to rebel against God. He refused to accept the fact that all of his greatness came from God. As his pride grew, Satan was determined to take over God's kingdom and seize control of His power. Thus Satan—the most beautiful, powerful, and wise of all created beings—started a war he could never win.

Because of His awesome holiness, God could not tolerate rebellion and evil in His kingdom. Therefore He stripped Satan of his position of authority, drove him from heaven, and disgraced him by throwing him to earth. Though this battle between God and Satan started in heaven, we are now caught right in the middle of it on earth. And because of Satan's great hatred and anger toward God, he is not about to let us walk away untouched by his fierce attacks and harassment.

The Nature of Satan

Now that we know more about Satan's true identity, we also need to know more about his character—what he is really like. The biblical names given to Satan provide us with further insight into his characteristics, background, looks, and even activities. Here's a brief look at the names of Satan, their meaning, and where in the Bible you can find them.

The Names of Satan*

Name	Meaning	Reference
Satan	"Adversary/opposer"	Zechariah 3:1; Matthew 4:10; Revelation 12:9; 20:2
Devil	"Slanderer"	Matthew 4:1; Ephesians 4:27
Evil one	"Intrinsically evil"	John 17:15; 1 John 5:18,19
Serpent	"Craftiness"	Genesis 3:1; 2 Corinthians 11:3
Serpent of old	"Deceiver in Eden"	Revelation 12:9
Great red dragon	"Fierce nature"	Revelation 12:3,7,9

The Names of Satan*

Name	Meaning	Reference
Abaddon	"Destruction"	Revelation 9:11
Apollyon	"Destroyer"	Revelation 9:11
Adversary	"Opponent"	1 Peter 5:8
Accuser of the brethren	Opposes believers before God	Revelation 12:10
Tempter	Entices people to sin	Matthew 4:3; 1 Thessalonians 3:5
Ruler of this world	Rules in world system	John 12:31
Beelzebub	"Chief of the demons"	Luke 11:15
Belial	"Worthlessness/ wickedness"	2 Corinthians 6:15
God of this world	Controls philosophy of the world	2 Corinthians 4:4
Prince of the power of the air	Control of unbelievers	Ephesians 2:2
Father of lies	Perverts the truth	John 8:44
Murderer	Leads people to eternal death	John 8:44
Angel of light	Imitates a "shining angel"	2 Corinthians 11:14

* The exact wording of the names and designations of Satan varies somewhat among various Bible translations.

Satan is also described in 1 Peter 5:8 as "a roaring lion looking for someone to devour." You might say that he is like a serial killer stalking his next victim. Nevertheless, there is no reason to live in constant fear of what the devil may do next, especially if you have a relationship with God through His son Jesus. God has not given us a spirit of fear, but rather one of power (2 Timothy 1:7). The Bible reminds us in 1 John 4:4 that "the one who is in you is greater than the one who is in the world." Don't forget that Satan is a created being and is therefore no match for Almighty God. When we have surrendered to Christ as Savior and Lord, we can have victory over the attacks of the devil and the forces of darkness.

Satan's Strategies

Because Satan was created above all others in intelligence, he is a brilliant war planner and has developed some clever deceptive strategies to use in his attacks against us. Let's take a closer look at these tactics so that we will not be caught unaware of the devil's crafty schemes.

Doubt. Satan wants to undermine God's character and credibility. He started this back in the Garden of Eden with Adam and Eve. Satan wanted them to doubt what God said and why He said it (Genesis 3). The devil wants us today to be uncertain of who God is and what He is like. Satan would also like us to be skeptical about the promises of God's Word and ultimately even doubt that we have a relationship with Him. Satan will do all he can to make us ineffective through doubt.

Yet remember that the Bible teaches that Satan is a liar (John 8:44) and that God is incapable of lying, according to Titus 1:2. When you struggle with doubt, think of the evidence in the past of God's faithfulness to you and others you know or have read about in the Bible. Get your eyes off any circumstances that may be causing you to doubt and instead put your eyes on the Lord. Make sure you saturate your heart and mind in God's word (Romans 10:17). For further study take a look at John 10:28 and James 1:5-8.

Difficulties. Satan wants to use difficulties and problems in our lives in order to discourage us. He will use everything possible against us to make things hard: stress at home with your family, pressure on the job, and strained relationships with friends. Sometimes it could even be a form of persecution on the job. Satan's adversity may even come from individuals within your extended family or church. He will try anything and everything to frustrate God's plan for your life. Ultimately the devil would like for you to get so discouraged that you turn your back on God and walk away from Him.

When the going gets tough, remember the promise Jesus gave us in John 16:33: "I have told you these things so that in me you may have peace. In this world you will have trouble. But take heart! I have overcome the world." No matter how bad things may seem to get, Jesus promises to never leave us or turn His back on us (Hebrews 13:5). Instead of asking God why these things may be happening to you, start asking Him how He wants to help you through this difficult time in your life. Here are some additional passages from the Bible to look at: John 15:18,19 and Romans 16:20.

Self-sufficiency. Satan wants us to trust in our own strength and resources, and not rely on God. He works hard at misleading us to place our confidence in the wrong things. This is sometimes reinforced by the messages we hear in the world, from a variety of sources—philosophies that go exactly opposite to what the Bible teaches. "Be all you can be," "You've come a long way," "The power is within you," and the list goes on and on. The devil works subtly to keep us off the "main road"—where God wants us—and instead make us think we can live independently of God.

Two of the key signs that the devil is using this tactic on you is when your prayer life becomes almost nonexistent and your time studying God's Word disintegrates into basically nothing. This self-reliance is really what the very core of sin is: attempting to live your life independently of God. Satan wants us to depend on ourselves and not on the resurrection power of Jesus Christ. However, God reminds us in John 15:5 that apart from Him we can do nothing.

The Lord wants us to rely upon Him for everything. He promises to provide for us no matter how bleak the situation may seem. When we need answers or have challenges to overcome in our life, we need to trust God. The apostle Paul reassures us that we can do everything through Christ, who gives us strength (Philippians 4:13).

A quick and easy way to find out just how self-sufficient you have become is to look at how much time you spend in prayer on a consistent basis and what you pray about. Here are some additional verses to look at: Psalm 84:5 and Proverbs 3:5,6.

False Teaching. The devil wants to frustrate and mislead us with false teaching. And it can come in many forms. For example, he uses rock stars who dedicate their albums to God but live like animals. Musicians are like preachers, but often with a different message to be sung.

He also uses well-meaning people who are members of false religions or cults who want us to believe that Jesus was just a good man or is reincarnated and back here on earth leading their particular group. Sometimes listening to false teaching can be deadly. Look at what happened in Waco, Texas, when over 80 people (including children) followed cult leader David Koresh to his death because he said he was God. I believe most of those people would still be alive today if they knew their Bibles better and recognized the lies of the enemy. Or what about those who were part of the "Heaven's Gate" cult in Southern California?

The problem is that we have strayed from the teaching of God's Word and are depending more on what people say than what God says. We are not spending enough time studying the Bible, so we don't know how to respond to the issues of life from God's perspective. Therefore we become easy targets of the enemy.

Remember, the primary way God communicates to you is through His written Word, the Bible. One of the marks of someone who is growing in his or her spiritual life is turning to the Bible frequently in their search for answers about life's questions. Don't neglect time studying God's Word. Here are some verses to get you started: Luke 6:47-49 and 2 Timothy 3:16,17.

Confusion. Satan is a master at confusing us with mixed messages. He has worked hard at eroding the moral standards our society once lived by. Whether dealing with sex outside of marriage, drugs, or alcohol, the messages are becoming more and more confusing: "Just say no," "Just wear a condom," "You can drink, just don't drive." Isn't it amazing how some of the celebrities appearing in ads designed to give society positive motivation are the very ones who violate their own advice!

Satan wants us to be so baffled about what is right and wrong that we will compromise our faith in Christ. When our life is in a blur it is much easier for him to mislead us. Living in a confusing world can be dangerous to our spiritual health. The prophet Isaiah described it this way: "Woe to those who call evil good and good evil, who put darkness for light and light for darkness, who put bitter for sweet and sweet for bitter" (Isaiah 5:20).

When you are feeling confused, just remember that our Father in heaven is not a God of confusion but one of balance, peace, hope, and love. Ask God for wisdom and direction for your situation. Pray to God then examine His Word for wisdom. Here are some promises you can count on: Isaiah 30:21 and Philippians 4:6,7.

The Reality of Demons

The Bible reminds us that this spiritual battle we are involved in includes not just Satan but demons as well. Without question the Bible affirms the reality of demons. Jesus confirmed their existence numerous times during His earthly ministry. (See Matthew 10:1; 12:22-29; 15:22-28; Mark 5:1-16; Luke 10:17.) All the writers of the New Testament (except the writer of Hebrews) mention demons. There are also many passages in the Old Testament where demons are referred to.

Demons are more than just figures of speech or concepts that merely exist in our minds. Moreover, they are not flesh and blood but are spirit beings, according to Ephesians 6:12. As "created beings" they are not present everywhere, yet they are not as restricted as human beings by the normal barriers of space.

Demons possess intelligence (Mark 1:24), emotions (Luke 8:28; James 2:19), a free will (Luke 8:32), and a personality (Luke 8:27-30). They can also possess superhuman strength at times, as with the demon-possessed man in the book of Mark (5:1-18). Having chosen to rebel against God with Satan, demons continue to oppose the purposes and plan of God in this world. In the process, they promote false religion (1 John 4:1-4; 1 Timothy 4:1-3) and the worship of idols (Leviticus 17:7; Deuteronomy 32:17; 1 Corinthians 10:20).

Be Prepared!

Satan's identity, his various names, and his strategies not only affirm the reality of his existence but also reveal the many-faceted aspects of his work. He is a powerful, intelligent, and clever creature, and we must never forget or underestimate the reality of our enemy nor his forces of darkness. Don't be deceived: The devil has a plan and a purpose for each person. For those without Christ, he will do all he can to keep them from surrendering to Jesus as Savior and Lord of their lives. It doesn't matter how much you go to church, seminars, or concerts, or even listen to Christian radio, as long as you don't open your heart to Christ.

Satan's plan for those who are Christians is to keep them from growing in the strength and knowledge of Jesus, as well as to keep them from telling unsaved family and friends that they too can find hope and abundant life in Christ.

More than anything, remember that Jesus is your advocate and that He defeated Satan on the cross at Calvary. And having disarmed the powers and authorities, he made a public spectacle of them, triumphing over them by the cross (Colossians 2:15). The devil is powerless in the presence of the Son of God. Ultimately Satan will be judged and cast into the lake of fire for eternity (Revelation 20:7-10).

Despite the problems and trials we may face in life, we are on the winning side with Christ as our Savior. God has given us all the necessary resources to withstand the attacks of the enemy, including special spiritual weaponry and equipment (see Ephesians 6:11-18). God's strategy for our victory is summed up in James 4:7: "Submit yourselves, then, to God. Resist the devil, and he will flee from you." So at Halloween time and throughout the year be prepared for spiritual battle.

PART THREE

What's a Christian Supposed to Do?

7

A View from the Book

onrad believes if you let your kids trick-or-treat, you'll go to hell. Seventy-five-year-old Angie remarked how her family celebrated Halloween growing up and it didn't affect them. Michael didn't see anything wrong with Halloween until he became a Christian. Cam does not want to promote Halloween in any way, not even an alternative. Penny likes to have praise parties for kids and encourages parents to meet for prayer on October 31. Wayne teaches 8–12-year-old boys in Sunday school and gives each one a special bag to use for trick-or-treating. And Charlotte puts a sign on her front door explaining why she doesn't believe in celebrating Halloween.

Knowing how to respond to contemporary culture issues like Halloween can be confusing and frustrating at times. Everyone has an opinion as to what he or she believes is the best thing for a Christian to do. After being interviewed dozens of times the last couple of years on various radio and television programs, I am convinced that I have heard the best and worst advice that people have to offer. But the bottom line in responding to any issue is not what other people think, no matter how adamant they may be that their opinion is right. All that matters is what God says in His Word.

The Bible is God's Handbook for living and as such it contains truth that needs to be examined in the light of topics like Halloween. That's why it is important to get a "view from the Book." There are no chapters and verses that you can turn to that specifically mention trick-or-treating, costume parties, or pumpkin carving. Yet there are solid principles which, if applied properly, can enable us to respond to the Halloween issue in a way that pleases God and is positive for our families.

Principles for Discerning

Back in the 1940s or '50s the world of the occult was still secretive and Halloween was viewed as an innocent children's activity. But times have changed. Today some Christians wonder whether it is still acceptable to participate in an activity, like Halloween, that has a degree of association with the occult. Rather than attempting to speculate about what is right or wrong with Halloween based purely on opinion, let's take a look at some timeless guiding principles from the Bible. These principles can also be applied to other issues of life in contemporary society.

1. *Not everything is constructive.* God has given each one of us a free will and the freedom to choose. Knowing how far to exercise this liberty can sometimes be difficult to discern, especially in things that the Bible is silent upon as to being right or wrong. The apostle Paul addressed this issue with the Corinthian church: "Everything is permissible, but not everything is beneficial" (1 Corinthians 10:23).

As Christians we have liberty in all things not specifically mentioned in the Bible as sinful. However, this freedom must be exercised in such a way as to build up our spiritual life and encourage others. Whatever contributes to spiritual growth is good and helpful. We must be careful when it comes to questionable things, the gray areas of life that are not specifically forbidden in the Bible. Often these gray areas have to do with contemporary culture issues like Halloween.

It's not hard to determine that believers should not actually celebrate Halloween, but what about the option of participating in an alternative? With all the publicity that Halloween receives, it does provide a good opportunity to turn on the light of God's Word through various types of alternatives, especially for kids. "Is it constructive?" "Is it good?" "Is it profitable?" should be our guiding principles for any alternative that we or our children participate in. Are there alternatives that Christians can participate in that are beneficial? Yes, there are. And of course, in Christ we also have the freedom *not to* participate in an alternate activity.

2. *Guard against unholy practices.* The occultic activities we discussed earlier in the book are still largely removed from the activity of current mainstream Halloween celebrations and parties. A parent should not be worried that he or she is supporting the occult by allowing his child to dress up as a clown or an angel to go trick-or-treating. Any authentic occult activities that are associated with Halloween in the collective public can be easily avoided. How can we be sure of what practices and activities should be avoided? Moses, writing in the Old Testament, provides a list for us.

> Let no one be found among you who sacrifices his son or daughter in the fire, who practices divination or sorcery, interprets omens, engages in witchcraft, or casts spells, or who is a medium or spiritist or who consults the dead. Anyone who does these things is detestable to the LORD, and

> because of these detestable practices the LORD
> your God will drive out those nations before you.
> You must be blameless before the LORD your God
> (Deuteronomy 18:10-13).

We live in a time when people are curious and fascinated with the things of the occult. Satan is behind the occult, and God warns us to stay away from such practices. It's not hard to see occultic influences in some Halloween costumes, games, and decorations. Use this list as a starting point for evaluating the way in which you or your children may be participating in a Halloween alternative.

Also carefully check around to see whether there are any occult-related items that may have innocently been brought into your house. It could be decorations, costumes, or even coloring books. A couple of years ago my mother bought our twins "Fun on Halloween" coloring books. Even though they were published by Creative Child Press, they were filled with witches, ghosts, poltergeists, goblins, and gnomes. The story line that corresponded with the pictures was about a brother and sister who fell victim to a spell and were trapped in their bedroom.

As innocent as things like this may seem, we must get rid of them so as to not have that influence in our homes. Remember, the devil often works subtly to gain a foothold in our lives.

3. *Stay focused on what is good and pure.* There is a battle raging today for the minds and emotions of our kids. But that battle is just as real for you and me. What we put into our minds determines what comes out in our words and actions. We must fill our minds with thoughts that are true and good and right. Paul's advice to the Christians at Philippi is just as relevant to us as we consider Halloween.

"Finally, brothers, whatever is true, whatever is noble, whatever is right, whatever is pure, whatever is lovely, whatever is admirable—if anything is excellent or praise-worthy—think about such things" (Philippians 4:8).

We must carefully examine what we and our children are putting into our minds through television, books, computer games, movies, and magazines. With network programmers pulling out all the stops at Halloween, television is a good place to start in guarding against harmful input. If you have questions about a television show, movie, cartoon, or comic book, compare it with the standards listed in this verse. When it comes to staying focused on what is good and pure, don't forget to be careful what you and your children are exposed to on the Internet.

Above all, read God's Word and pray. Ask Him to help you focus your mind on what is good and pure. It takes practice, but it can be done.

4. *Sidestep all evil.* Evil is pervasive in our society today. And it appears to be more noticeable during Halloween than at other times of the year. This is not to say that evil doesn't exist at other times, but just that people seem to demonstrate their fascination with evil more during Halloween celebrations and festivities. Some take it to extremes, while others just see how "close they can get to the fire" without getting burned. But God is very clear in His word what His attitude is toward evil: "Avoid every kind of evil" (1 Thessalonians 5:22).

In one sense, a Christian can no more avoid all evil than a boat can avoid all water. He can, however, make sure his "boat" has no leaks. Evil is everywhere today, and you don't have to go very far to see it. As we mentioned in an earlier chapter, it has permeated so much of our society today that people have become desensitized to it.

Ultimately, evil should never be allowed into a Christian's heart. Whether advice or any other form of evil, all of it must be avoided. As we also learned in a previous chapter, evil can be enticing and seductive. Those with inquisitive minds could begin to wonder whether witches, ghosts, and other related Halloween characters have any power, and from there begin to explore and experiment. For some people Halloween could become a gateway to the occult—their first step into the world of darkness.

When giving thought to Halloween and participating in an alternative, everything from masks to games to decorations must be carefully evaluated. God wants us to hold ourselves free from the influence of evil, even in entertainment and recreation. Instead of seeing something that the world might see as "cute," we need to look at it through the filter of God's Word. Then we will be able to avoid even the appearance of evil.

5. *Be aware of the battle.* One of Satan's most effective strategies—and therefore a great danger to believers—is the deception that there exists no serious threatening conflict between good and evil in the supernatural realm. Some would naïvely argue that there appear to be many good things happening in the world today. But the Bible is clear that the war between God and Satan has not diminished but intensified, including its front on this earth.

"For our struggle is not against flesh and blood, but against the rulers, against the authorities, against the powers of this dark world and against the spiritual forces of evil in the heavenly realms" (Ephesians 6:12).

In this verse Paul reminds us that the Christian struggle is not only against Satan but also against a host of his subordinates, who like the devil himself are not flesh and blood. They are not mere fantasies, but are very real. Our greatest enemy is not the world we see, corrupt and wicked as it is, but the world we cannot see.

Paul's purpose here is not to explain in great detail the demonic hierarchy but to give us some idea of its sophistication and power. We are up against an incredibly powerful evil and potent enemy. Nevertheless, our need is not to recognize every feature of our adversary but to turn to God, who is our powerful and reliable source of protection and victory.

Halloween is said to be the highest of holy days for Satanists. Some of the recognized tools of Satan worshipers during Halloween are witches, wizards, sorcery, amulets, talismans, vampires, incantations, the practice of necromancy, and blood sacrifice. Ancient Druids believed that "All Hallows Eve" (October 31) was when the "Lord of Death" summoned all souls of evil people who had been condemned to death to inhabit the bodies of animals. Even though much of this is far removed from the mainstream of Halloween festivities today, we still must be aware of Satan's schemes and attacks—not just during Halloween, but the rest of the year as well. We cannot allow ourselves to become complacent and oblivious to the seriousness of the battle all around us.

Our responsibility is to resist and stand firm. The issue is not what we go out and do, but rather, when the battle is over and the smoke clears, whether we are found standing true to Jesus. Peter counsels us to be "self-controlled and alert. Your enemy the devil prowls around like a roaring lion looking for someone to devour. Resist him, standing firm in the faith" (1 Peter 5:8,9).

As you turn to God's Word for guidance on Halloween—or any other contemporary issue—you must remember to guard against twisting it in any way to support a preconceived opinion. "Correctly handle the word of truth" as the apostle Paul advised young Timothy in 2 Timothy 2:15.

This was not meant to be an exhaustive list of guiding principles from God's Word regarding Halloween. There are many more verses that would be just as relevant and practical. Still, the previous section does provide a good foundation for getting started in how best to respond to cultural issues like Halloween.

Respecting Different Opinions

Because Halloween falls into the gray area of Christian living that is not specifically forbidden in the Bible, we must recognize that there will be differing opinions on how to respond to it. That is why we must carefully assess the circumstances involved and be willing to respect someone else's opinion that may differ from ours. Essentially, there will be times when we must "agree to disagree" with other believers on a subject like Halloween. When this occurs, we should be willing to allow for and respect the differences of opinion.

Ultimately, it all comes down to being careful not to compromise biblical principles in your own life as you respond to issues in contemporary culture. First Corinthians 10:31 summarizes it in this way: "So whether you eat or drink or whatever you do, do it all for the glory of God." This is the supreme test that every believer should apply to his life. The Lord must so permeate our lives that all we do is for His glory, even in the most mundane, routine, nonspiritual things of life such as eating and drinking. His glory is to be our life commitment. It should be the purpose of our whole life, which belongs to the Lord because we have been "bought at a price" (1 Corinthians 7:23). A person lives a life that either honors God or dishonors Him.

When considering how you will respond to Halloween (or any other contemporary culture issue), keep this as a guiding principle: "Is this glorifying to God? How can I glorify God through this?" Whatever a Christian does should be done in such a way as to glorify God, and responding to the issue of Halloween is no exception. God's Word is always the standard by which we measure all things, both the mundane and the not-so-mundane. It is and always will be our Handbook for living.

Halloween ABCs

The woman was calling from Othello, Washington, and even over the phone I could tell she was upset by the tone of her voice. Her concern was over a book called *Halloween ABC*, published by Macmillan Publishing Company, that was being used as part of the curriculum in the local elementary school. She asked if I would do a review of the book that she could bring to the school board. After receiving a copy of the book, I was shocked not only by the content but also by the fact that it was being used to teach young children the alphabet. Here are a few examples from the book:

> A is for Apple
> Apple, sweet apple, what do you hide?
> Wormy and squirmy, rotten inside.
> Apple, sweet apple, so shiny and red,
> taste it, don't waste it, come and be fed.
> Delicious, malicious;
> One bite and you're dead....

> D is for Demon
> Diabolic demons dance in the dell,

> diabolic demons cast their spell;
> Make this spot infernally hot,
> put your hate in, Satan;
> Pass the pitchfork, please, Mephistopheles;
> Lucifer, Beelzebub, come when we call.
> The devil, the devil, the devil with it all.

I is for Icicle
> An icy stabbing so swiftly done,
> the victim scarcely felt it.
> The police are baffled: "Where's the weapon?"
> The sun shines down to melt it.

After reviewing the book, several questions came to my mind, especially in light of Webster's definition of the word "educate": What is this material really teaching? What knowledge and skills are being instilled, and what character qualities could possibly be reinforced with this content? Not only were the descriptions of each letter filled with occultic overtones, but the illustrations also contained satanic symbols. Without question this book falls short of even the most basic standards of education for a grade-school child.

The Change in Public Education

Our sixth-grade son, Tony, came home from school on October 31 with a copy of a word bank quiz he had taken that day in one of his classes. It was titled "The Story of Halloween." The content dealt with Halloween's origin, ghosts, evil spirits, and traditions in New Zealand, England, and Australia. We were proud of him for getting 100 percent on the quiz, but would have much preferred that he be studying something more productive.

Public education has changed dramatically in the last two decades. Gone are the days of the traditional three "R's"—reading, 'riting, and 'rithmetic. A fourth "R" has now been added—reproductive rights. Schools have become battlefields for a wide array of causes and issues—school-based clinics, values clarification, evolution, self-esteem, and gay awareness. The dropout rate is increasing, and we are just beginning to wake up to the literacy problem.

During hearings held by the U.S. Department of Education on proposed regulations for the Protection of Pupil Rights Amendment, over 1300 pages of testimony were recorded by court reporters as public school teachers, parents, and concerned adults recounted their eyewitness accounts of the psychological abuse of children in the public school system. Accounts were given of how classroom instruction has confused kids about life, standards of behavior, moral choices, religious beliefs, and relationships with peers and parents.[19] Kids are being alienated from their parents and traditional morality, while being taught to rationalize rather than discern. We've certainly come a long way since the little red schoolhouse.

Abraham Lincoln once said, "The philosophy of education in one generation will be the philosophy of government in the next." Public education influences the greatest number of people in the most thorough way at the most impressionable age. Just what philosophy are our children being taught in the classroom today? What values are they assimilating to help them deal with the passages of life?

Concerned parents across America are rising up to take action against the significant inroads into the educational system that the occult and the New Age movement have made. We cannot completely comprehend the impact this movement is having on the educational process until we understand the many faces the New Age is wearing in schools today. The real purpose behind exposing schoolchildren to the occult was summed up by a teacher attending a New Age seminar: "To help the children get in touch with their divinity. These things are crucial to our own evolution."[20]

A New Age in the Classroom

The U.S. Army Research Institute asked the National Research Council to form a committee to assess the field of techniques that purport to enhance human performance. The members were drawn from The National Academy of Sciences and Engineering and the Institute of Medicine.

Many of the techniques under consideration grew out of the Human Potential movement of the 1960s, including guided imagery, meditation, biofeedback, neurolinguistic programming, and various other techniques to reduce stress and increase concentration.[21] The Army, like many other institutions, is attracted to the prospect of cost-effective procedures that can improve performance. Educators are looking for the very same thing to enhance classroom performance, and New Age researchers are all too anxious to install their methodology in the classroom. Let's take a brief look at some of the things that are transpiring in some classrooms today.

Schools are gradually replacing education that addresses a child's intellect by teaching knowledge and skills (cognitive) with education that targets the child's feelings and attitudes, spending classroom time on psychological games (affective). This new direction has been dubbed "therapy" education by some. A new jargon has even been designed by those who promote therapy education. This educational language includes phrases like "values clarification," "behavior modification," "moral reasoning," "higher critical thinking skills," and "holistic education." Techniques associated with these phrases are being carefully integrated into school curricula. New Age methodology such as yoga, meditation, and globalism is also being masked by terminology that doesn't sound quite so strange or threatening, so as to not alarm parents and essentially hide the truth of what is being taught.

This apparent innocence of New Age terminology makes the basic ideas easily acceptable. New Age activist Dick Sutphen states: "One of the biggest advantages we have as New Agers is once the occult, metaphysical, and New Age terminology is removed, we have concepts and techniques that are very acceptable to the general public. So we can change the names to demonstrate the power. In doing so, we open the door to millions who normally would not be receptive."[22]

According to Professor Allan Bloom, "Courses in value-clarification teach kids to discover and clarify their own values rather than having them imposed by outside authority. Those that are springing up in schools are supposed to provide models for parents and encourage kids to talk about things like abortion or sexism—issues the significance of which they cannot possibly understand. Such education is little more than propaganda. Propaganda that does not work, because the opinions or values arrived at are will-o'-the wisps, insubstantial, without ground in experience or passion, which are the basis for moral reasoning. Such values inevitably change as public opinion changes."[23]

Values clarification is compatible with New Age thinking on "confluent education." This New Age theory posits the equality of individual values because everyone has the wisdom of the universe within. New Age proponent and actress Shirley MacLaine puts it this way: "We already know everything. The knowingness of our divinity is the highest intelligence."[24]

A New Journey?

Jack Canfield, Director of Educational Services for Insight Training Seminars, is a strong proponent of "holistic education." In his paper titled "The Inner Classroom: Teaching with Guided Imagery" he states: "Guided imagery is a very powerful psychological tool which can be used to achieve a wide variety of educational objectives: enhance self-esteem, expand awareness, facilitate psychological growth and integration, evoke a more positive attitude, and accelerate the learning of subject matter."

Canfield concludes his paper to teachers with these thoughts: "I hope you will attempt some of the suggestions I have presented you with here. If you do, you will embark upon a new and adventurous journey in your teaching. You can expect some profound changes to occur in your classroom, and in these days of stress and burnout, that's a nice thing to look forward to."[25] Unfortunately, many teachers have no idea what they are really involved with, but are simply going along in ignorance. Teachers themselves are being led in these various techniques so as to experience firsthand the wonders they will be exposing their kids to.

Many teachers today are being encouraged to transform their classrooms into laboratories to experiment on children rather than to emphasize basic life skills. Kids are at a crucial stage of life when values, perspectives, and morals are under attack from TV, the print media, and now in their own classroom. What was once supposed to be a safe haven of learning has turned into an occultic minefield of indoctrination and conversion. Transcendental Meditation practices are now being used under the guise of increasing self-esteem. Astrologers, palm readers, channelers (mediums), and even Tibetan monks are being invited to come into classrooms to "challenge students," all in the name of critical thinking and understanding a different worldview.

Teachers are being shown how they can make use of fantasy role-playing games to enhance performances. One such game, "The Wizard," is being played in some class-rooms as part of the curriculum. Kids are taught to cast spells on each other. The described purpose of the game is to progress from one "spelling power" level to the next. Humans are at the lowest end of the spectrum, having very limited powers, and are at the mercy of monsters. Higher levels include enchanters, sorcerers, magicians, and of course the Wizard.

In some schools kids are routinely sent to the school counselor's office to lie on the floor and breathe deeply. Then they meditate as they listen to a series of guided fantasy tapes, while they empty their minds and at times are even led to participate in astral projection.[26]

Textbooks and Curriculum

As we saw with the book *Halloween ABCs*, long gone are the days of "Dick and Jane." No longer are primary school children being taught to read from innocent materials. They have been replaced with books containing stories that promote fear, violence, and occultic themes. This becomes even more horrifying to think about when you realize the power that these textbooks have to influence the vulnerable minds of our children. Seventy-five percent of students' classroom time and 90 percent of their home-work time is spent with textbook materials.[27]

The National Institute of Education commissioned a systematic study of the content of public school textbooks. The conclusion was rather alarming: "Religion, traditional family values, and conservative political and economic positions have been reliably excluded from the children's textbooks."[28] Any educator can tell you that omitting these values from textbooks sends a very definite message to children: "These values must be unimportant because they were omitted. They are of lesser value than those which were included."

New Age educators are developing and testing curriculum materials at a feverish pace in hopes of gaining acceptance in school districts across the country. In order to be approved, the curriculum is being cleverly disguised and packaged as brain research and "scientific" techniques to help develop creativity, enhance learning capacity, and enable children to manage stress, solve problems, and improve their self-esteem. How does the curriculum measure up to these rather lofty goals? Let's take a look at excerpts from the *Impressions* series published by Holt Rinehart and Winston of Canada, and you judge for yourself.

- First-graders are asked whether they would rather be "crushed by a snake, swallowed by a fish, eaten by a crocodile or sat on by a rhinoceros."

- Second-graders see a drawing of a green creature whose long, sharp claws are gripping the head of a small child.

- *Under the Sea*, a third-grade reader, features an innocent-looking illustration titled "Shut the Windows, Bolt the Doors." The illustration shows floating objects: a refrigerator, a stove, a teddy bear, and a slice of pie. The teacher's manual instructs the educator to assign children the task of composing a spell. They are to write and chant a spell to make things in the room float and then do the same thing to return the room to normal.

Accompanying this reader is a student workbook that includes an exercise entitled "Three Spells." One spell it teaches is "Zap." This spell creates a blast of lightning that shoots from the caster's hand. It is effective against virtually all living creatures that have no magical defenses.[29]

Much of this material is from the milder U.S.-Calgary version of *Impressions*. Other versions that exist are the Canadian, the U.S.-Canadian, and the Calgary. Many of the editions sold in the United States during the last few years are the darker and scarier U.S.-Canadian version.

Mission SOAR

Mission SOAR (Set Objectives, Achieve Results) was piloted in the Los Angeles School District to help reduce gang violence and build self-esteem in kids. They were taught to "communicate with the dead" and receive "guidance" from their "spiritual guides" on how to plan their future lives. Mission SOAR very closely parallels the techniques found in *Beyond Hypnosis: A Program for Developing Your Psychic and Healing Powers,* by William W. HeWitt.[30]

Children who are talented and gifted are of prime interest for "conversion" to New Age philosophy. Because these programs are generally very open for experimentation, gifted-and-talented programs become prime avenues for occult-oriented "transpersonal education" to enter the classroom. After all, what better place to work out all the "bugs" before introducing the material into the mainstream of the educational process?[31] "Flights of Fantasy" is a program used with gifted children. It is a form of guided imagery that trains children to imagine meeting strange creatures in space and then encourages the children to join or merge with them before returning to earth.

There is no doubt that this material is damaging to the young minds who are subjected to it under the guise of public education. As you examine some of these examples closely, you begin to realize that most of the content is too much for a young child's psyche to process. The frightening imagery overwhelms them as they are being asked to deal with issues that they are ill-equipped to handle. And in the process of study they are being desensitized to the things of the occult and New Age. It is this subtle desensitization that we must protect our kids against.

Occultic Influence in Education

Let's examine some of the potential threats of occultic influence in the educational process of children.

1. Confluent education leads kids to believe that they are divine and perfect. Since the sin problem is non-existent, there is no need for Jesus Christ and what He accomplished on the cross. Because the kids are taught they are godlike, they develop a false sense of confidence.

2. The use of guided imagery in the classroom teaches children a way of dealing with problems that leaves God out of the picture. It can also open them up to "angels of light" (2 Corinthians 11:14).

3. New Age visualization is dangerous because it denies the lostness of man or the sin problem. Remember that our imaginations were affected by the fall of man (Genesis 3:1-7; 6:5).

4. Values clarification in the classroom denies the existence of moral absolutes deriving from the Bible. Instead, each student is encouraged to come up with his or her own moral value system.

5. Eastern meditation teaches one to empty the mind with the goal of attaining oneness with all things—a "cosmic consciousness." Biblical meditation is much different because it always has an objective focus—filling the mind with the Word of God.

With confluent education, guided imagery visualization, values clarification, Eastern meditation, and a variety of mystical and occultic curricula making their way into schools, it becomes clear that the New Age movement has made significant inroads into the educational system. Thus there are profound implications for Christian parents who have children in public schools.

Be on Guard!

The apostle Paul encourages believers in 1 Corinthians 16:13,14 to be on guard and stand firm in the faith and to "do everything in love." It is important to keep these principles in mind as you develop a plan for guarding your child's education. Here are some basic things to consider.

1. *Stay informed.* It has been said that the best defense is a good offense. The main problem is that most parents don't have a clue as to what is going on in their children's schools. Find out if your child's class is having a Halloween party and what they do there. Contact your local school district office and ask what curriculum is being used. Ask permission to review the material for yourself. If your request is denied, file a complaint with the district. And do your homework. Know what you're talking about; don't go to the school without a factual, well-thought-out defense. It will only make matters worse. Earn the right to be heard.

2. *Get involved.* It's not enough to be involved in cake sales and school field trips. Parents need to go beyond "meeting their obligations" by merely helping out at school occasionally. Get into the classroom. Observe what is taking place. Inform the teacher and administration if you notice any questionable practices going on. Again, remember to "stand firm" but "do everything in love." It does take time—valuable time—but it's worth the investment.

3. *Gather support.* Seek out curriculum experts, child psychologists, teachers, other parents, pastors, and others who share your views. Develop a united group to request a meeting with the superintendent to discuss the curriculum and questionable activities in the classroom. Be persistent. And most important, pray.

4. *Take action when necessary.* If the teacher, administration, or superintendent rejects or ignores your request, or if you have a one-sided and unproductive meeting, consider going to the school board. Prepare well and document everything in writing, with actual copies of offensive materials where possible. If it appears that harmful curricula or practices will remain, request that alternative classes be established for children whose parents are opposed. Ask that a parental review panel be established to monitor quality control in these alternative classes.

Let's do something before we lose another generation. We've already lost one and cannot bear to lose another. Do not allow the complacency of our society to subtly restrain you. There is too much at stake and we can ill afford to allow themes of despair, occultism, mutilation, and witchcraft to deeply entrench themselves in the vulnerable minds of our children.

9

Why Should the Devil Have All the Fun?

here will come a time in the life of every parent when he or she will have to decide what to do with Halloween. For some it will come sooner rather than later, but eventually there will be a day of decision. What is the right thing to do with this fall holiday that is gathering more and more attention each year? Is there severe judgment awaiting the parent who allows his or her child to trick-or-treat? If you don't celebrate Halloween, are there any other options? Whose advice should you listen to?

There's always plenty of advice to be found when it comes to hot topics such as Halloween, and often you can get your fill by listening to radio talk shows. Remember Phil, in chapter five, the guy from Toronto who decided to share his two-cents' worth on the "Lifeline" show where I was a guest on Halloween? He was convinced that if everyone just ignored the Halloween holiday, it would eventually disappear.

What Are Our Options?

Unfortunately for Phil, he doesn't realize that Halloween is here to stay, and that burying our heads in the sand won't make it go away. So if ignoring Halloween is not going to work, what are some valid options that we can consider?

The first option is to simply not participate in anything at all associated with Halloween. This means locking your front door, turning out the light, and basically acting as if no one is home when trick-or-treaters come through your neighborhood. One lady told me she leaves the porch light on and puts a sign on her front door each year that reads: "Our family does not participate in Halloween. Have a safe return home. God bless you."

This is certainly a valid option, but it does present a problem that will need to be dealt with if you have younger children. Because Halloween is such a big retail holiday and celebrations have crept into our schools, kids will want to know why they can't do what their friends at school and in the neighborhood are doing on Halloween. This is definitely not an insurmountable problem, but there is even a bigger issue that we need to think about.

Let's look at the big picture for a minute. Because Halloween is such huge business, there is a lot of publicity and attention given to October 31. Why not take advantage of all this fanfare and use it to "turn on the light" of God's Word with an alternative that could take people one step closer to a relationship with Jesus? Ephesians 5:16 encourages us to "make the most of every opportunity," and Halloween is just such an occasion for Christians who are serious about making a difference in their world.

Remember that participating in an *alternative* is not the same thing as celebrating the *holiday*. When we celebrate a holiday, like Halloween, we are publicly bringing some sort of honor to the day. When we participate in an alternative, we are taking part in providing a choice between Halloween and some other event. We can choose to be part of an alternative to Halloween without the stigma of expressing some type of satisfaction with the traditional celebration of the holiday. The right alternative can be safe and fun for kids and yet still honor God. It's important that our kids do not feel as if they are missing out on something just because they are Christians. Ultimately, Halloween can be a great opportunity to "overcome evil with good" (Romans 12:21).

Many Shapes and Sizes

Alternatives to the typical Halloween celebration can come in many different shapes and sizes. They are limited only by your sense of imagination and creativity. The alternative doesn't have to be complex or expensive; it all depends on what you want to accomplish and the amount of time you are able to invest. For some parents it will be as simple as planning a special family night on October 31. This could be a great time to establish some fun family traditions. Start by serving a favorite meal for dinner, then plan an evening of fun activities and games just for the kids. You could also plan to go out somewhere as a family and finish off the evening at home with a special dessert.

There are many other ways that Christians can respond to Halloween. Here are some other alternatives for you to consider.

1. *Reverse door-to-door evangelism.* Most of us are familiar with Christians going door-to-door to tell others about Jesus and distribute tracts and literature. In our neighborhood we are frequently visited by Christians from different churches, as well as members of religious cults distributing their literature. In the last couple of years some churches in our area have also adopted the *Jesus* video project. This strategy includes giving neighbors a free copy of the video

to watch. A return trip to the same house is made at a later date to discuss the film with members of the household.

As a Halloween alternative, take this same concept and reverse it. Instead of you going to someone else's house, take advantage of the fact that trick-or-treaters automatically come to your door. When you answer the door, give them some candy and a Christian tract on fear or some other topic related to Halloween. Imagine being able to be involved in door-to-door evangelism without ever leaving your home!

2. *Reformation Day costume party*. On October 31, 1517, Martin Luther is credited with spearheading the Protestant Reformation. Some historians believe that, next to the introduction of Christianity, the Reformation was one of the greatest events in all of history. The early cries for reformation (restoration of biblical Christianity) were heard through the pounding of Martin Luther's hammer on the chapel door of Wittenburg University in Germany. The 95 theses (short statements) he nailed to the door proved to be the catalyst for a new direction in evangelical thinking. Some of Luther's theses were written against the religious practice of people making a monetary payment in order to be set free from eternal punishment for sin. Implicit in his writings was the concept of salvation by grace alone. October 31 thus became known as Reformation Day.

Invite children to come to your home or church dressed as biblical characters for a party. Have a contest and award prizes for the most creative costume, funniest, etc. Games and refreshments will add to the festivities and party atmosphere. Also include a time to briefly explain what the Reformation was and the impact it had on the history of the church. As you explain the concept of God's grace and salvation, you will also have a great opportunity to give children a chance to establish a personal relationship with God through receiving Christ. Your pastor or church library may also have some books that can provide more specific information for this part of the event.

3. *Harvest Festival.* A number of churches in our area host a special harvest event on Halloween night. Children from the neighborhood are invited to attend a festival of games, contests, and refreshments. Candy is given out at each booth or game and children are encouraged to attend wearing nonghoulish costumes or ones that represent a Bible character. One church even has a "trunk-or-treat" in the parking lot. People open the trunk of their car and fill it with candy, and then children from the neighborhood get "treats" by walking through the safety of the church parking lot. Another church provides free bags for trick-or-treating as well as maps to church members' houses where they will receive a "special treat."

4. *Progressive dinner.* Help the youth group at your church put together a progressive dinner. Encourage the kids to come dressed in costumes, then transport them from home to home with a different food course at each location. Also plan a stimulating game for each home, then finish the evening back at the church for dessert and a short devotional talk on evil, the occult, or a related topic.

When it comes to alternatives to Halloween, teenagers are often left out or forgotten. Because we are dealing with a generation that is apathetic, fascinated with evil, and searching for power, we need to make sure that we give these kids wholesome options to the parties that kids at school host on Halloween. It may take a bit more work to put something together for older kids, but it's worth it.

Pete Ryder, a friend of mine who is a youth pastor in Kansas, has a "Harvest Bash" for his youth group on Halloween. Their activities include bobbing for potatoes in mashed potatoes, a nongory costume party, a food-game team competition, a pumpkin-decorating contest, a team cheer, a caramel-apple race, and a devotion on wearing masks and disguises from 1 Samuel 16:7. In the past, Pete has also had a "Harvest Family Day," with fun activities, for positive family interaction.

If you're really ambitious you may want to encourage your church to plan a special outreach concert for youth on Halloween. Whatever you do, make sure it is fun and relevant for "Generation Next."

If you decide to plan an alternative for your children and their friends, remember to use the Bible as your filter for what takes place at the event. The worst thing you could do is to present an option to kids that is just like every other Halloween event in town. In your planning don't see how closely you can copy the world; instead, make it appealing but different. Whatever you do, remember the principle found in l Corinthians 10:31: "Whether you eat or drink or whatever you do, do it all for the glory of God."

Our desire should be to please God in everything we do, and a Halloween alternative is no exception. We can provide a fun and safe option to Halloween for kids and in the process still glorify God. Why should the devil have all the fun? Let's be creative as we turn on the light of God's Word and overcome evil with good on October 31.

10

Parenting in a Seductive Age

There is a battle raging today for the minds and emotions of our kids. So much is coming at them from so many different directions. Life is complex and confusing for today's kids, let alone their parents. They have shapable minds and soft hearts. They are individuals with a tremendous spiritual hunger seeking help and hope to navigate through the enticements of contemporary culture.

Halloween is just one of the many current issues that demands strong and thoughtful parental guidance. It's not easy being a parent in the shadow of the twenty-first century. As concerned parents and adults, what can we do to protect our kids in this seductive age?

Everyone knows that parenting is risky business. There are no "money-back" guarantees that all will turn out well for our children. However, God does promise us in Proverbs 22:6 that if we point our kids in the right direction, when they're old they won't wander around aimlessly. The key to raising healthy kids in a seductive age is based on taking God's Word seriously and applying it to every dimension of life. It is practical, timely, and relevant to all the issues of life, including how we should respond to Halloween.

Before we examine some practical parenting advice for the twenty-first century, let's first take a quick look at how we can realistically keep children safe on Halloween.

Halloween Safety Is No Trick

For many children, especially younger ones, Halloween can be a potentially frightening time, especially with its occultic shadowings and nightmarish overtones.

Trick-or-treating has come a long way since Irish and Scottish immigrants introduced Halloween customs to America in the 1800s. While begging for candy may still be practiced in some rural areas, the trend has subsided in suburban areas. Trick-or-treating began to taper off in large cities during the mid-1900s because many neighbors did not know one another. Today, house-to-house visits by trick-or-treaters have given way to more organized and safer events.

The move toward organized Halloween activities was tracked in a national survey conducted by the Opinion Research Corporation. The poll focused on 500 families nationwide with children younger than 11. Thirty-four percent of the families surveyed indicated they would be spending Halloween with friends and family in festive celebrations. That marked an 8 percent increase in parties over the past five years. Forty-one percent said they would visit only friends' houses, opting to pass by the homes of unfamiliar neighbors. This figure represents an 18 percent increase for this type of visit over the preceding five years. An explanation for the shift toward alternative celebrations was given by 32 percent of those surveyed, who favored a safer Halloween for children.[32]

In considering the health and physical safety of children on Halloween, here are several suggestions to keep in mind if you choose to take your child trick-or-treating or to an alternative activity.

1. Make sure your children are wearing warm clothes under their costumes.

2. Only allow them to wear costumes made out of fire-retardant material. Also make sure the costumes are loose enough to allow freedom of movement, but short enough so the child won't trip. Believe it or not, falls are the leading cause of accidents on Halloween. And don't forget to decorate costumes with reflective tape or some sort of glow-in-the-dark tape.

3. Be sure that costume accessories such as swords, canes, and saber lights are made with flexible materials.

4. Make certain that masks have adequate openings for the nose, mouth, and eyes for safe vision and breathing. Likewise make sure to use only safe and washable face makeup and body paints.

5. Supply a small flashlight for your child, as well as light-colored or luminous bags to collect their treats in.

6. Work out the trick-or-treating route and times in advance. Emphasize safety rules regarding traffic and strangers. And most important, plan on walking the appointed course with your kids, especially if they are under 12 (if they are over 12, send them in groups). This makes trick-or-treating more of a family activity and provides a better measure of safety as well.

7. Emphasize to your child the importance of bringing candy home for inspection before eating any of it.

Then make sure that you sort through the goodies and throw away anything dubious.

The one key element overarching all these suggestions is your commitment as a parent. Comedian Bill Cosby in his book *Fatherhood* said, "I've chosen to be involved in the raising of my children." As parents, we must make a commitment to be actively involved in the lives of our children. And the more involved we become, the more time we must sacrifice. Just remember that parenting will always cost you something, whether you pay now or pay later. The difference is that if you wait until later, it's always more costly. Now let's take another look at the topic of time commitment as well as some other ideas for parenting in the twenty-first century.

Practical Tips for Parenting

In a book this size we cannot go into the depth I would like to in discussing parenting. However, I will offer you some basic and practical tips on raising kids in a society that at times is both seductive and consumed with evil. These ideas are foundational for understanding your kids and building healthy relationships with them. Be careful of merely glancing through the following material as just a review of things you already know. The real issue is whether you are actually *practicing* them.

1. *Get in touch with your kids.* All too frequently I find that parents know more about their ancestral history than they do about the activities of their own children. That's why an important element of parenting is getting a grasp on the likes, dislikes, and lifestyles of our kids. This can only happen when we make a conscious effort to invade their world and counter their culture. Without this hands-on knowledge it's tough to earn the right to be heard and talk with our children. In our position as parents we can attempt to

enforce our right to be heard, but this is never as effective as earning it.

In 1 Corinthians 9:22 we find some advice that can be applied to this very element of parenting: "When I am with those whose consciences bother them easily, I don't act as though I know it all and don't say they are foolish; the result is that they are willing to let me help them. Yes, whatever a person is like, I try to find common ground with him so that he will let me tell him about Christ and let Christ save him" (TLB). The apostle Paul gives several important principles for parenting: Establish common ground with your kids; avoid a know-it-all attitude; learn from your kids about their world; let your kids know that you accept them; be sensitive to their needs and concerns; and most important, look for opportunities to live out and share your faith with your kids.

2. Learn to listen. Kids today need their parents to do more than just "hear them out." They need moms and dads who will actually listen to them. Webster's dictionary defines listening as "to hear with thoughtful attention." Do you really listen to your kids? How about your spouse?

Once again the Bible provides us with some relevant counsel on this aspect of parenting. Proverbs 18:13 says, "He who answers before listening—that is his folly and shame." Sometimes it is easy to advise or correct your child in a given situation before you have really heard with careful attention what he or she has to say. This takes time and work, but it sure beats becoming like the person who is always saying, "Don't confuse me with the facts!"

James 1:19 offers this advice for parenting: "Everyone should be quick to listen, slow to speak and slow to become angry." This verse encourages parents (and others) to put a mental stopwatch on their conversations and to keep track of how much they talk and how much they listen. Listening demonstrates to our kids that we think what they have to say is important. It can also help curb unnecessary anger eruptions.

3. *Work at understanding.* Do you really comprehend the challenges your kids are facing today, especially the older ones? Forty percent of kids surveyed say that their views are either ignored or bypassed. So they conclude that their parents don't really care. Our ability to grasp our kids' outlook about different issues in life enables us to better demonstrate our care and concern for them. Learning to understand is foundational to positive relationships with your children.

At the core of understanding are two important concepts. First, as parents we must become thoroughly familiar with the personality and disposition of each of our children. Second, we must work at putting ourselves in the position of our children and thereby gaining more insight about the world in which they live. When speaking to parents I often comment to them, "I know you're aware that it is the '90s, but do you realize that it's the 1990s?"

Things are markedly different today from when we grew up. Certainly there are similar problems as with previous generations, such as drug and alcohol abuse, premarital sex, and teenage rebellion, but the problems facing kids today are more complex and the intensity is greater than in any previous generation. That's why it is important for parents today to put themselves in their children's place. A lot of the strain between parents and kids nowadays could be reduced through better communication and understanding. It's been said that home is not where you live but where they understand you.

Proverbs 11:12 reminds us that a person of understanding holds his tongue. How many times have you said something you regretted right after the words rolled out of your mouth? Imagine how different our family life might be if we as parents worked harder at understanding our children and their perspective before we spoke. Earlier in this chapter we talked about the importance of earning the right to be heard with our kids. According to Proverbs 13:15, good understanding wins favor. Gaining favor with our children through understanding can help us navigate through a multitude of child-rearing issues.

4. *Love them genuinely.* Everyone believes love is important, but we usually think of it as just a feeling. In reality genuine love is a choice and an action, as 1 Corinthians 13:4-7 shows: "Love is very patient and kind, never jealous or envious, never boastful or proud, never haughty or selfish or rude. Love does not demand its own way. It is not irritable or touchy. It does not hold grudges and will hardly even notice when others do it wrong. It is never glad about injustice, but rejoices whenever truth wins out. If you love someone you will be loyal to him no matter what the cost. You will always believe in him, always expect the best of him, and always stand your ground in defending him" (TLB).

These verses offer us a great checklist to examine the kind of love we demonstrate toward other members of our family. Our kids need this kind of love if they are going to survive in a seductive culture. However, the kind of love the Bible is talking about is not humanly possible without divine help. God is the source of our love: He loved us enough to sacrifice His only Son for us, taking the punishment for our sins. Jesus is the ultimate example of what it means to love; everything He did in life and death was supremely loving. The Holy Spirit gives us the power to love. God's love always involves a choice and an action, and our love for our children should be like His.

Putting It All Together

Parenting is never easy. It takes time, energy, and effort. Halloween is just one of many on a long list of parenting challenges in a seductive age.

In the last 20 years we have seen increased spending on education and social welfare, parents are better-educated, and families are smaller—yet our children are at greater risk than ever before. Why? A major contributing factor is a generation of parents who are unwilling to spend time building the lives of their children. There is no substitute for sharing our lives with our kids. After all, many kids today spell love T-I-M-E.

Ultimately, if we want our children to survive in this seductive age, we must not only spend time building their lives, but we must also help them develop a vital, personal relationship with Jesus Christ. He is our strength, hope, and peace in a confused world that has lost its way. Don't assume that your child is a Christian simply because *you* are a Christian and have taken him to Sunday school on a regular basis. He must make a personal commitment of his life to Jesus Christ as Savior and Lord, and who better to lead him to that commitment than his parent? Here are a few important guidelines for leading your child to Christ.

Pray for your child's salvation. You can't argue your child into becoming a Christian, but you can pray for him and allow God to prepare his heart to receive the gospel. Your child's salvation should be at the top of your prayer list.

Tell stories. Kids often understand concepts better when they are presented through stories. Tell or read your child Bible stories about people who were challenged to surrender their lives to Christ. For example, you might consider using: Jesus talks with Nicodemus (John 3) or Jesus and Zacchaeus (Luke 19). Also, expose your child to good Christian children's books that present God's love and His plan for salvation.

Give a simple gospel presentation. At some point you must clearly and lovingly share the gospel with your child and invite him to surrender his life to Jesus. There are many excellent tracts available which summarize the gospel in terms a child can understand. Whether you use one of these tools or not, your presentation should include these basic truths:

- God loves you and wants to give you peace as well as eternal and abundant life (John 3:16; 10:10; Romans 5:1).

- You are sinful and separated from God (Romans 3:23; 6:23).

- Jesus paid the penalty for your sin when He died on the cross (John 14:6; Romans 5:8).

- You must confess your sin and receive Jesus Christ as Savior and Lord (John 1:12; 1 John 1:9; Revelation 3:20).

As you talk with your child about spiritual matters, be sure to speak at his level. Don't use "Christianese" or abstract theological terms ("saved," "repent," "justification," etc.) without thoroughly explaining their meaning in words your child can understand. Also, don't try to scare or manipulate your child into making a response. Simply present the gospel, answer his or her questions, and allow the Holy Spirit to bring him to the point of deciding to trust Christ.

Give a clear invitation. After you have explained the plan of salvation and are convinced that your child understands it, say something like, "Would you like to receive Jesus right now?" If he responds negatively, accept his decision and continue to pray for him and share the gospel with him. If he says yes, lead him in a simple prayer by having him read it aloud or repeat it after you phrase by phrase. Here is a sample prayer you can use:

> Dear Jesus, I know I have sinned and need Your forgiveness. I now turn from my sins to follow

You. I believe that You died on the cross for my sins and that You came back to life after three days. I invite You to come into my heart and life. I want You to be my Savior and Lord. Thank You for Your love and the gift of eternal life. In Your name I pray. Amen.

Review his decision. After leading your child in a prayer of salvation, take a few minutes to talk through the following questions with him to help him understand what has happened:

What did you just do? Say?

What did Jesus do when you opened your heart to Him? (See Revelation 3:20.)

What did you become when you received Jesus into your heart? (see John 1:12)

Where is Jesus right now?

A Final Challenge

Perhaps you have been reading about leading your child to Christ but have not personally received Christ yourself. Remember, Jesus died for both children and adults. If you have never surrendered your life to Christ, why not take a few minutes right now to pray the simple prayer suggested above? Committing your life to Christ is the most important thing you will ever do. There is no greater joy than knowing God personally. And by the way, if you or your child receive Christ as a result of this book, please drop us a note, using the address in the back of the book. We'd like to pray with you and send you some information on how to begin this new relationship with Jesus.

One last thing. Remember that the best thing we can do as parents is to pray with and for our children. Take a few minutes right now to pray for each one of your children.

Ask God to protect them and to give you the wisdom and understanding necessary to effectively parent in a seductive culture.

Now What Am I Supposed to Do?

Since you've made it to this point in the book, one of two things has happened: Either you've finished this volume after diligently reading through it or you've jumped ahead to look for an exciting conclusion! If you made the effort to faithfully read each chapter, now I would like you to take a few minutes for personal reflection and application.

It would be so easy to set this book on the shelf and move on. However, that was not my intent in writing it. My desire is that this material would motivate you to "do something"—practically apply the information—to your own situation as a concerned parent or adult. To do this effectively will require some time on your part, but I believe it will be worth every minute invested.

Take the time to review each chapter, using the brief outline and questions I have provided for you in this section of the book. With some chapters you will have received content that was more informative than practical.

Regardless, take the time to reflect and apply anyway; it can't hurt. But in most cases I think you should be able to find at least one concept that you can practically apply to your parenting circumstances.

If you are married, you may want to discuss these thoughts together with your spouse. If you are a parent, for some chapters I've included discussion questions for you to use with your children. When it comes down to real application in daily living, remember the phrase that Michael Jordan and other mega-athletes have made famous the world over: "Just do it!"

Halloween Then and Now (Chapter 1)

- What surprised you the most about the history of Halloween?

- Do you recognize any remnants from ancient pagan festivals in the way Halloween is celebrated in your community?

- What do you know about the Protestant Reformation?

Costumes, Tricks, and Smiling Pumpkins (Chapter 2)

- What Halloween traditions did you practice as a child?

- Have you continued to carry on some of these same practices with your own children? Why or why not?

- How important do you feel it is to develop family traditions at Halloween time?

For Children

- What do you like most about Halloween? Least?

- Are there certain costumes that God would not want you to wear? Why?

- What would you like to see your family do on Halloween?

Witches, Ghosts, and Things That Go Bump in the Night (Chapter 3)

- In light of Galatians 5:19,20, take a few minutes to carefully evaluate your own life. If you are caught in the trap of one or more of these sins, confess it to God and seek His forgiveness. Don't let unconfessed sin create a barrier between you and your heavenly Father.

- Do you have a friend or family member who is messing around with witchcraft? Besides praying for him, how else can you practically help him?

For Children

- Children today are very vulnerable to witchcraft, which is prevalent in today's media. Set aside some time with your child to discuss things they may have seen on television or heard about at school. Then use all or some of the following passages as discussion points to help them understand what God wants us to do regarding witchcraft: Deuteronomy 18:9-13; 2 Kings 9:22; Nahum 3:4; Micah 5:12; Revelation 21:8.

Evil Goes Mainstream (Chapter 4)

- How do you most frequently come in conflict with the world? What do you need to do so you won't be so vulnerable to this temptation?

- Have you ever faced an incident in your life when you were tempted to leave God out for a period of time? What happened?

- How would you describe your relationship with God? How would *He* describe it?

Everybody's Doing It (Chapter 5)

- How did your family observe Halloween when you were growing up?

- In what ways have you noticed that Halloween has changed in the last few years?

- What do you think Jesus would do with Halloween?

For Children

- What would Jesus want you to do on Halloween?

- Describe the most unusual Halloween decoration you have ever seen. Did you like it? Why or why not?

- What bothers you the most about the way most people celebrate Halloween?

Satan Surfs the Internet (Chapter 6)

- What strategy does the devil most often use in your life? Why? What does God want you to do in this area of your life to achieve victory?

- List some specific examples of false teaching that you have noticed in the world. How can you best prepare yourself to be on guard against these subtle attacks?

- How does the conflict between God and Satan express itself in your life? Be specific.

For Children

- Talk with your child about the reality of God and Satan in the world today (make sure it is age-appropriate). Use the biblical names of the enemy as a foundation for your discussion. Remind your child that God is all-powerful in the spiritual battle, and that when they feel afraid they should call on the name of Jesus for help.

  Note: For additional help in this area check out my book, *The Seduction of Our Children*, published by Harvest House.

A View from the Book (Chapter 7)

- Has my response to Halloween in the past glorified God?

- What guiding principle do I most need to apply in my life?

- Is there someone that I need to "agree to disagree with" on how I respond to Halloween?

For Children

- Read Philippians 4:8. How does this apply to Halloween?

- In what ways can we honor God on Halloween (see 1 Corinthians 10:31)?

- Discuss with your children, in a way that is appropriate for their age, the presence of an all-powerful God and His enemy, Satan, in our world today. Make sure you explain how God protects us and why it is important to trust Him.

Halloween ABCs (Chapter 8)

- When was the last time you visited your child's school?

- How well-informed are you about what takes place in the classroom?

- Do you pray with your children before they go to school?

For Children

- What do your teachers at school say about Halloween?

- Do you like the way your classroom is decorated? Why or why not?

- What do some of your friends at school say about Halloween?

Why Should the Devil Have All the Fun? (Chapter 9)

- What was the key thought in this chapter?

- What is your position on Halloween?

- What are you going to do differently this year?

Parenting in a Seductive Age (Chapter 10)

- Are there any changes you need to make regarding your child's safety at Halloween?

- In what way can you demonstrate love to your child in the next week?

- Which of the practical parenting tips need more work in your life?

For Children

- If you could dress up as any character, who would you be?

- What is your favorite thing to do at school? Why?

- Who is your best friend? Why?

What Should We Do?

As you continue to give consideration as to how you and your family will respond to Halloween, try to approach the issue as levelheaded and biblically-based as possible. Keep in mind that just because there are pagan elements in the early history of Halloween, this does not mean that it automatically disqualifies a Christian from participating in some form of alternative. As we have learned in previous sections of this book, God certainly does not want us to be associated with these early pagan practices. But He does want us to take advantage of every opportunity to share the gospel, and Halloween is a great time to do that because of all the heightened attention given to the things of darkness.

Also keep in mind that many American holidays, customs, and traditions have pagan remnants in their history. It would be pretty tough to say that participating in these holidays would be wrong simply because of early pagan associations. Easter and Christmas are two examples of holidays that were derived from pagan celebrations. It is interesting to note that down through history the church has appropriated these and others and made them "Christian."

For example, Easter involved a pagan fertility ritual. The Christmas tree apparently originates from the ancient European idea that evergreen trees embody powerful spirits. Fertility rites and sacrifices were associated with mistletoe. Birthday cakes most likely originated from offering cakes and candles to Artemis, the ancient Greek god of the hunt and the moon. The idea of June brides is related to "Juno," the Roman goddess of marriage, who presided over the month of June. Even the days of the week are named after pagan gods. Monday is "moon day," Wednesday refers to "Woden's day," Thursday refers to "Thor's day," and Saturday refers to "Saturn's day."

And even though the remnants of ancient paganism still endure, the practices and anti-Christian beliefs once associated with Easter and Christmas, as well as other holidays and customs, have long ago disappeared. Who would even dream of not using his or her monthly planner because of the name origins of the days of the week? What would a birthday party be without a cake and candles? Can you imagine not celebrating our Lord's resurrection on Easter Sunday because of a fertility ritual? That would be crazy!

Our Responsibility As Christians

When it comes to Halloween, even though it has occultic associations, the way in which most people use it should not determine our attitude toward the holiday. For the average person it is purely a secular "party day" that can be participated in without any occult connections. Our responsibility as Christians is twofold.

First, whatever we do on or around Halloween should glorify God. We should not compromise biblical values in any way. A word of caution here: The values of Christians are not always biblically based values. So just because someone in your church participates in Halloween in a particular way does not make it right for you. Don't forget that Halloween falls into the gray area of Christian living not specifically forbidden in the Bible. Always be aware that there will be differing opinions in the church community on how a Christian should respond. And be careful as you exercise your Christian freedom regarding Halloween, so that you don't become a stumbling block to others who are weaker in the faith (1 Corinthians 8:9).

Second, we should take advantage of all the publicity about and around Halloween to tell others of the true source of power and the One who can enable us to celebrate all year long—Jesus! There has never been a more opportune time in history to tell others about the source of "abundant life," yet it is estimated that less than 3 percent of believers ever share their faith. We live in a world that has lost its way, and people are desperately seeking hope and help like never before. There is a tremendous spiritual hunger with the generation of today, and we have the answer in Jesus Christ.

There are also certain times of the year when people are more curious about the supernatural, and Halloween is one of them. So let's follow Paul's advice in Ephesians 5:16 and make "the most of every opportunity" by taking advantage of the massive attention our society gives to Halloween. Let's look for creative ways to tell others that God is alive and still in the business of changing lives!

Appendix A

Satanic/Occultic Symbols

 Anarchy. Represents the abolition of all law and the denial of authority. Initially, those into punk music used this symbol. Now it is widely used by the followers of heavy metal music and self-styled Satanists.

 Ankh. An ancient Egyptian symbol of life often associated with fertility. The top portion represents the female, and the lower portion symbolizes the male.

 Anti-justice. The Roman symbol for justice was an upright double-bladed ax. The representation of anti-justice inverts the double-bladed ax.

  Black Mass indicators. These signs can be used as a source of direction as well as a sign of involvement in Black Masses.

Blood ritual. Represents human and animal sacrifices.

 Cross of confusion. An ancient Roman symbol questioning the existence or validity of Christianity.

 Cross of Nero. Represented peace in the '60s. Among today's heavy metal and occult groups it signifies the defeat of Christianity (an inverted cross with the cross anchor broken downward).

 Diana and Lucifer. The moon goddess Diana and the morning star Lucifer are found in nearly all types of witchcraft and Satanism. When the moon faces the opposite direction, it is primarily a satanic symbol.

 Hexagram. Also referred to as the seal of Solomon, the hexagram is said to be one of the most powerful symbols in the occult.

 Horned hand. A sign of recognition among those in the occult. It is also used by those attending heavy metal concerts to affirm allegiance to the music's message of negativism.

 Mark of the beast. Four different representations of the mark of the beast or Satan. Note that the letter F is the sixth letter in the alphabet.

Pentagram. A five-pointed star, with or without the circle, is an important symbol in most forms of magic. Generally, the top point represents spirit and the other points represent wind, fire, earth, and water.

Sample altar. The altar may be any flat object where the implements of the ritual are placed. Usually the altar will be placed within a nine-foot circle. It could be as large as 48 inches long, 22 inches wide, and two inches high. The pentagram in the center is etched into the slab. Human or animal blood is then poured into the etching. Other symbols may be carved according to individual group traditions. Implements on the altar may include: chalice, candles, parchment, cauldron, and the Book of Shadows. A smaller version of the altar can be found in the bedrooms, closets, etc. of young, self-styled Satanists or dabblers.

Swastika (broken cross). A symbol of ancient origin, it originally represented the four winds, the four seasons, and the four points of the compass. The swastika represents the elements or forces turning against nature and out of harmony. Neo-Nazis and occult groups use it in this manner.

Talisman or amulet. An object with the name or image of a god drawn or inscribed in it.

 Triangle. May vary in size, but it is generally inscribed or drawn on the ground as the place where a demon would appear in a conjuration ritual.

 Upside-down pentagram. Sometimes called a baphomet, it is strictly satanic and represents a goat's head.

Appendix B

Satanic/Occultic Terms

Amulet. A charm or ornament supposedly charged with magical power and used to ward off spells, disease, and bad luck.

Ancient one. A name sometimes given to an officiating priestess at a Black Mass.

Arcana. A secret process or formula. In tarot, 22 cards comprise the Major Arcana and 56 cards divided into four suits are the Minor Arcana.

Athame. A dagger or ceremonial knife used to cast a circle and perform other witchcraft rituals. It is one of the basic tools of witchcraft.

Baculum. A witch's wand, staff, or broomstick.

Black Mass. Held in honor of the devil on the witches' Sabbath. The ritual reverses the Roman Catholic mass, desecrating the objects used in worship. Sometimes the participants drink the blood of an animal during the ceremony. Often a nude woman is stretched out on the altar, and the high priest concludes the ritual by having sex with her.

Book of Shadows. Also called a grimoire, this journal is kept either by individual witches or Satanists or by a coven to record the activities of the group and the incantations used.

Cantrip. A spell cast by a witch.

Chalice. A silver goblet used for blood communions.

Charm. Chanted or spoken words used to invoke a spell, or an object said to have supernatural power.

Circle. The space within which wiccan rituals are held and where it is believed that contact with greater spiritual forces can be achieved.

Coven. A group of Satanists who gather to perform rites. There are traditionally 13 members, but with self-styled groups the number varies. A coven is also called a clan.

The Craft. Witchcraft.

Curse. Invocation of an oath associated with black magic or sorcery intended to harm or destroy property or opponents.

Demon. To occultists, any nonhuman spirit; according to the Bible, an angel who rebelled against God.

Dianic. The Dianic cult worshiped a two-faced, horned god known to the Romans as Janus or Dianus and who represented the cycle of seasons. This was supposed to be the ancient religion continued by covens of witches. Today the Dianic tradition refers to the related worship of the triple goddess—maiden, mother, and crone.

Druids. A branch of dangerous and powerful Celtic priests from pre-Christian Britain and Gaul who are still active today. They worship the sun and believe in the immortality of the soul and reincarnation. They are also skilled in medicine and astronomy.

Esbat. A coven meeting held at regular intervals, such as once a week or at some phase of the moon.

Familiar. A demonic spirit who serves a witch or medium.

Grove. A group of covens.

Lady. A female leader of a coven.

Ligature. A spell which prevents a person from doing something.

Magick. Magic that employs ritual symbols and ceremony, including ceremonial costumes, dramatic invocations to gods, potent incense, and mystic sacraments.

Magic circle. A circle inscribed on the floor of a temple for ceremonial purposes. Often nine feet in diameter, it is believed to hold magical powers within and to protect those involved in the ceremony from evil.

Magister. The male leader of a coven.

Magus. A male witch.

Materialization. The (apparent) physical manifestation of a spirit being.

Necromancy. A practice in which the spirits of the dead are summoned to provide omens for discovering secrets of past or future events.

Necrophilia. An act of sexual intercourse with a corpse.

Occult. From the Latin *occultus,* meaning "secret" or "hidden." The occult refers to secret or hidden knowledge available to initiates, to the supernatural, and sometimes to paranormal phenomena and parapsychology.

Omen. A prophetic sign.

Poltergeist. Comes from two German words: *polter* (to make noise by throwing or tumbling around) and *geist* (ghost or spirit). The literal translation for the term is "noisy ghost."

Ritual. A prescribed form of religious or magical ceremony.

Runes. A northern European alphabet used by occult groups in secret writing. There are several forms of runering.

Sabbat. A quarterly or semiquarterly meeting of witches or Satanists.

Santeria. A mingling of African tribal religions and Catholicism established by African slaves brought to the Americas and the Caribbean.

Seal. A demon's summoning diagram or signature.

So mote it be. Words spoken at the end of an occult ceremony. Similar to "amen" in traditional religious services.

Sorcery. Magic, usually of the black variety.

Spiritism. Seeking guidance from dead persons contacted through mediums.

Talisman. A power object, usually an amulet or trinket.

Voodoo. An ancient religion combining ancestor worship, sorcery, charms, and spells. Those involved are extremely superstitious and are heavily involved in using strange objects to worship.

Warlock. Often used for a male witch, but it actually designates a traitor.

Wicca. The pagan end of the witchcraft spectrum.

Witch. A male or female practitioner of any sort of witchcraft.

White magic. Magic that is supposedly helpful or beneficial.

Witchcraft. Known as the "Old Religion," it is an ancient practice dating back to biblical times. It is defined as the performance of magic forbidden by God for nonbiblical ends. The word "witchcraft" is related to the old English word "wiccan," the practice of magical arts, occultic arts, and nature worship.

Appendix C

Pagan Festivals

There are eight pagan festivals in a given year. They are as follows:

Halloween (October 31). Halloween is the end and beginning of the witch's year. It marks the beginning of the death and destruction associated with winter. At this time the power of the spirit world is unleashed and spirits are supposedly free to roam about the earth. Halloween is considered the best time to contact spirits.

Candlemas (February 2). Candlemas was a celebration of lengthening days and the soon coming of spring.

Beltane (April 30). Beltane or Walpurgis Night roughly coincides with the time for planting crops. The Celts and others also offered sacrifices at this time.

Lammas (July 31). Lammas occurs about the time when fruits and vegetables are ripening and the harvest season is beginning.

Yule (December 22). Yule is the winter solstice, or shortest day of the year.

Vernal Equinox (March 21). Day and night are the same length, with the days getting longer.

St. John's Eve (June 22). St. John's eve or midsummer is the summer solstice or the longest day of the year.

Michaelmas (September 21). The autumnal equinox, when day and night are the same length, with the days getting shorter.

Note: The names and dates of pagan holidays may vary according to information sources.

The early Catholic Church established opposing holidays to substitute for the pagan holidays. For example, in the spring, Easter replaced the vernal equinox and Walpurgis Night; in the summer, Assumption Sunday and Purification Sunday replaced St. John's Eve and Lammas; in the fall, All Saints Day replaced Halloween; and in the winter, Christmas celebration replaced Yule and Candlemas.

Appendix D

New Age Terms

Age of Aquarius. Astrologers believe that evolution goes through cycles directly corresponding to the signs of the zodiac, each lasting approximately 2000 years. Advocates of the New Age say we are now moving in the cycle associated with Aquarius. The Aquarian Age will supposedly be characterized by a heightened degree of spiritual or cosmic consciousness.

Akashic records. Assumed vast reservoir of knowledge. Some New Agers believe that the events of all human lives have been recorded in the Universal Mind or Memory of Nature in a region of space known as the ether.

Alchemy. Often associated with medieval folklore, this is a chemical science and speculative philosophy designed to transform base metals into gold. It is figuratively used regarding the change of base human nature into the divine.

Altered states. States other than normal waking consciousness, such as daydreaming, sleep-dreaming, or hypnotic trance; meditative, mystical, or drug-induced states; or unconscious states.

Ascended Master. A highly evolved individual no longer required to undergo lifetimes on the physical plane in order to achieve spiritual growth.

Aura. An apparent envelope or field of colored radiation said to surround the human body and other animate objects with the color or colors indicating different aspects of physical, psychological, and spiritual condition.

Biofeedback. A technique using instruments to self-monitor normally unconscious involuntary body processes, such as brain waves, heartbeat, and muscle tension. As this information is fed to the individual, he or she can consciously and voluntarily control internal biological functions.

Channeling. A New Age form of mediumship or spiritism. The channeler yields control of his perceptual and cognitive capacities to a spiritual entity with the intent of receiving paranormal information.

Chakras. The seven energy points on the human body, according to New Agers and yogis. Raising the kundalini through the chakras is the aim of yoga meditation. Enlightenment (samadhi) is achieved when the kundalini reaches the "crown chakra" at the top of the head.

Clairaudience. The ability to hear mentally without using the ears.

Clairvoyance. The ability to see mentally beyond ordinary time and space without using the eyes. Also called second sight.

Consciousness. Mental awareness of present knowing. New Agers usually refer to consciousness as the awareness of external objects or facts.

Consciousness revolution. A New Age way of looking at and experiencing life. The primary focus of the new consciousness is oneness with God, all mankind, the earth, and the entire universe.

Cosmic consciousness. A spiritual and mystical perception that all the universe is one. To attain cosmic consciousness is to see the universe as God and see God as the universe.

Crystals. New Age advocates believe that crystals contain incredible healing and energizing powers. Crystals are often touted as being able to restore the flow of energy in the human body.

Dharma. Law, truth, or teaching. Used to express the central teachings of the Hindu and Buddhist religions. Dharma implies that essential truth can be stated about the way things are, and that people should comply with that norm.

Divination. Methods of discovering the personal, human significance of present or future events. The means to obtain insights may include dreams, hunches, involuntary body actions, mediumistic possession, consulting the dead, observing the behavior of animals and birds, tossing coins, casting lots, and reading natural phenomena.

Esoteric. Used to describe knowledge that is possessed or understood by a select few.

ESP. Extra-sensory perception. The experience of or response to an external event, object, state, or influence without apparent contact through the known senses. ESP may occur without those involved being aware of it.

Gnosticism. The secret doctrines and practices of mysticism whereby a person may come to the enlightenment or realization that he is of the same essence as God or the Absolute. The Greek word gnosis means "knowledge." At the heart of gnostic thought is the idea that revelation of the hidden gnosis frees one from the fragmentary and illusory material world and teaches him about the origins of the spiritual world to which the gnostic belongs by nature.

The Great Invocation. A New Age prayer that has been translated into over 80 languages. The purpose of this prayer is to invoke the presence of the cosmic Christ on earth, thus leading to the oneness and brotherhood of all mankind.

Harmonic convergence. The assembly of New Age mediators at the same propitious astrological time in different locations to usher in peace on earth and a one-world government.

Hologram. A three-dimensional projection resulting from the interaction of laser beams. Scientists have discovered that the image of an entire hologram can be reproduced from any one of its many component parts. New Agers use the hologram to illustrate the oneness of all reality.

Higher self. The most spiritual and knowing part of oneself, said to lie beyond ego, day-to-day personality, and personal consciousness. The higher self can be channeled for wisdom and guidance. Variations include the oversoul, the superconsciousness, the atman, the Christ (or Krishna or Buddha) consciousness, and the God within.

Humanism. The philosophy that upholds the primacy of human beings rather than God or any abstract metaphysical system. Humanism holds that man is the measure of all things.

Human Potential movement. A movement with roots in humanistic philosophy that stresses man's essential goodness and unlimited potential.

Initiation. An occult term generally used in reference to the expansion or transformation of a person's consciousness. An initiate is one whose consciousness has been transformed to perceive inner realities. There are varying degrees of initiation, such as first degree, second degree, etc.

Inner self. The inner divine nature possessed by human beings. All people are said to possess an inner self, though they may not be aware of it.

Interdependence/interconnectedness. Used by New Agers to describe the oneness and essential unity of everything in the universe. All reality is viewed as interdependent and interconnected.

Karma. The debt accumulated against the soul as a result of good or bad actions committed during one's life (or lives). If one accumulates good karma, he supposedly will be reincarnated to a desirable state. If one accumulates bad karma, he will be reincarnated to a less desirable state.

Kirilian. A type of high-voltage photography using a pulsed, high-frequency electrical field and two electrodes between which are placed the object to be photographed and an unexposed film plate. The image thereby captured is purported to be an aura of energy emanating from plants, animals, and humans that changes in accordance with physiological or emotional shifts.

Kundalini. A psychospiritual power thought by yogis to lie dormant at the base of the spine. The kundalini is believed to be a goddess and is often referred to as "serpent power."

Magic circle. A ring drawn by occultists to protect them from the spirits and demons they call up by incantations and rituals.

Mantra. A holy word, phrase, or verse in Hindu or Buddhist meditation techniques. A mantra is usually provided to an initiate by a guru who supposedly holds specific insights regarding the needs of his pupils. The vibrations of the mantra are said to lead the mediator into union with the divine source within.

Monism. Literally means "oneness." In a spiritual framework it refers to the classical occult philosophy that all is one: All reality may be reduced to a single unifying principle partaking of the same essence and reality. Monism also relates to the belief that there is no ultimate distinction between the creator and the creation (pantheism).

Mysticism. The belief that God is totally different from anything the human mind can think and must be approached by a mind without content. Spiritual union or direct communion with ultimate reality can be obtained through subjective experience such as intuition or a unifying vision.

New Age movement. The most common name for the growing penetration of Eastern and occultic mysticism into Western culture. The words New Age refer to the Aquarian Age which occultists believe is dawning, bringing with it an era of enlightenment and peace. Encompassed within the New Age movement are various cults which emphasize mystic experiences.

Nirvana. Literally a blowing out or cooling of the fires of existence. It is the main term in Buddhism for the final release from the cycle of birth and death into bliss.

Numerology. The analysis of hidden prophetic meanings of numbers.

Pantheism. The belief that God and the world are ultimately identical, that all is God. Everything that exists constitutes a unity, and this all-inclusive unity is divine. God is equated with the forces and laws of the universe but is not a personal being.

Paradigm shift. Refers to a shift in worldviews. The so-called new paradigm (new model or form) is pantheistic (all is God) and monistic (all is one).

Planetization. New Age advocates believe that the various threats facing the human race require a global solution called planetization. It refers to the unifying of the world into a corporate brotherhood.

Psi. The twenty-third letter of the Greek alphabet. A general New Age term for ESP, psychokinesis, telepathy, clairvoyance, clairaudience, precognition, and other paranormal phenomena that are nonphysical in nature.

Psychic. A medium, "sensitive," or channeler. Also refers to paranormal events that can't be explained by established physical principles.

Psychic birth. A quickening of spiritual or cosmic consciousness and power. This new consciousness recognizes oneness with God and the universe. Psychic birth is an occult counterpart to the Christian new birth.

Psychokinesis (PK). The power of the mind to influence matter or move objects (see also telekinesis).

Reincarnation. The belief that the soul moves from one bodily existence to another, until (usually after many lives) it is released from historical existence and absorbed into the Absolute.

Right-brain learning. The right hemisphere of the brain is believed to be the center of intuitive and creative thought (as opposed to the rational nature of the left hemisphere). New Agers have seized on this as a justification to bring right-brain learning techniques into the classroom. These techniques include meditation, yoga, and guided imagery.

Seance. A gathering of people seeking communication with deceased loved ones or famous historical figures through a medium.

Self-realization. A synonym for God-realization. It refers to a personal recognition of one's divinity.

Shaman. A medicine man or witch doctor.

Spirit guide. A spiritual entity who provides information or guidance, often through a medium or channeler. The spirit provides guidance only after the channeler relinquishes his perceptual and cognitive capacities into its control.

Syncretism. The fusion of different forms of belief or practice; the claim that all religions are one and share the same core teachings.

Synergy. The quality of "whole making"; the New Age belief in the cooperation of natural systems to put things together in ever-more-meaningful patterns.

Third eye. An imaginary eye in the forehead believed to be the center of psychic vision.

Tantra. A series of Hindu or Buddhist scriptures concerned with special yogi practices for swift attainment of enlightenment; also the practices, techniques, and traditions of these teachings.

Telekinesis. A form of psychokinesis (PK); the apparent movement of stationary objects without the use of known physical force.

Trance. An altered state of consciousness, induced or spontaneous, that gives access to many ordinarily inhibited capacities of the mind-body system. Trance states are generally self-induced.

Visualization. Also known as guided imagery; refers to mind over matter. Visualization is the attempt to bring about change in the material realm by the power of the mind.

Yoga. Literally, yoking or joining; any system or spiritual discipline by which the practitioner or yogi seeks to condition the self at all levels—physical, psychical, and spiritual. The goal of the Indian religious tradition is a state of well-being, the loss of self-identity, and absorption into the Absolute or Ultimate Being.

Yogi. A master of one or more methods of yoga who teaches it to others.

Zen. A type of Buddhist thought best known for its emphasis on breaking down the commitment and attachment to the logical and rational ordering of experience.

Zodiac. The imaginary belt in the heavens that encompasses the apparent paths of the principal planets except Pluto. Divided into 12 constellations or signs based on the assumed dates that the sun enters each of these "houses" or symbols, the zodiac is used for predictions in astrology.

Notes

1. Jack Santino, ed., *Halloween and Other Festivals of Death and Life*, (Knoxville, TN: University of Tennessee Press, 1994), p. 12.
2. Sue Ellen Thompson and Barbara W. Carlson, *Holidays, Festivals, and Celebrations of the World Dictionary* (Detroit: Omnigraphics, 1994), p. 132.
3. *Daily Bulletin*, Ontario, California, Nov. 2, 1997, p. A19.
4. Santino, *Halloween*, p. 24.
5. *Los Angeles Times*, Nov. 2, 1990, p. A21.
6. Lesley Pratt Bannatyne, *Halloween: An American Holiday* (New York: Facts on File, 1990), p. 124.
7. *Sassy*, "Witchcraft Is a Religion," March 1992, pp. 64-65, 80-81.
8. Ibid.
9. Ibid.
10. *The Daily Bulletin*, Aug. 20, 1993, p. G6.
11. *The Hot 200* (New Song Publishing, 1987), p.7.
12. ABC NEWS 20/20, Dec. 4, 1992.
13. Ibid.
14. Kurt Snibbe in the *San Bernardino Sun*, Oct. 26, 1995, p. D8.
15. Kent Salas in the *Daily Bulletin*, Oct. 30, 1994, p. B10.
16. Gene Sloan in *USA Today*, Sep. 26, 1997, p. 13D.
17. Candy Hainer in *USA Today*, Oct. 23, 1997, p. D1.
18. George Barna, *The Barna Report* (Ventura, CA: Regal Books, 1991) pp. 204-05.

19. Phyllis Schlafly, *Child Abuse in the Classroom* (Crossway Books, 1985), p. 11.
20. Johanna Michaelsen, *Like Lambs to the Slaughter* (Eugene, OR: Harvest House, 1989), p. 43.
21. Daniel Druckman and John A. Swets, *Enhancing Human Performance* (Washington D.C.: National Academy Press, 1988), p. 3.
22. Walter Martin, *The New Age Cult* (Minneapolis: Bethany House, 1989), p. 63.
23. Allan Bloom, *The Closing of the American Mind* (Simon & Schuster, 1987), p. 61.
24. Russell Chandler, *Understanding the New Age* (Word, 1988), p. 154.
25. Jack Canfield, *The Inner Classroom: Teaching with Guided Imagery* (1981).
26. Lori Ann Pardau and Timothy A. Bittle, "What Is Johnny Being Taught?" in *California Capitol Report*, as quoted in *Citizen Magazine* (Focus on the Family, Jan. 1990), p. 4.
27. Mel and Norma Gabler, *What Are They Teaching Our Children?* (Victor Books, 1985), p. 22.
28. Paul Vitz, *Censorship: Evidence of Bias in our Children's Textbooks* (Servant, 1986), p. 1.
29. Deborah Mendenhall, *Nightmarish Textbooks Await Your Kids*, as quoted in *Citizen Magazine* (Focus on the Family, Sep. 17, 1990), pp. 2-3.
30. Bob Simonds in *Citizens for Excellence Newsletter*, May 1990, pp. 2-5.
31. William G. Sidebottom and Frank York, *They Teach New Age in New Mexico's Schools*, as quoted in *Citizen Magazine*, July 1985, p. 10.
32. Steve Ray Linam, "Halloween Safety Is No Trick," in *Daily Bulletin*, Oct. 30, 1994, p. B10.

For information on how to purchase additional book and tape resources by Steve Russo, as well as information on the Real Answers radio program, newsletter, or fact sheets, or information on seminars, school assemblies, or crusades, contact:

Real Answers with Steve Russo
P.O. Box 1549
Ontario, California 91762

(909) 466-7060
Fax (909) 466-7056
e-mail: realanswers@linkline.com

You can also visit our web site at:
www.realanswers.com

Other Harvest House Reading

The Seduction of Our Children
Neil T. Anderson and Steve Russo

This provocative book will equip you to overcome the spiritual conflicts facing young people. It will also help you strengthen family bonds and defeat Satan's influence during these challenging days.

The Facts on Halloween
John Ankerberg and John Weldon

Is Halloween an innocent harvest celebration, or does it have a darker side? Bringing the history and practices of Halloween to light, this booklet will help determine your own approach to this holiday.

The Facts on the Occult
John Ankerberg and John Weldon

What is the occult and how influential is it in modern America? Do some people have latent psychic abilities? What are the physical, psychological, and societal consequences of engaging in occult practices? How does one find deliverance? This booklet tackles these and other tough questions about the occult and its growing influence on our lives.

Occult Invasion
Dave Hunt

Occult influences march freely in America today, infiltrating schools, organizations, homes, and even churches. How can you recognize what come from the occult? Noted cult and prophecy expert Dave Hunt exposes how the occult is invading our world through spirit communications, extraterrestrial phenomena, and hypnosis. Discover how holistic health and some "Christian" psychology practices have occultic overtones and how the New Age quest to play God is fulfilling prophecy by ushering in a one-world religion.

Also by Steve Russo...

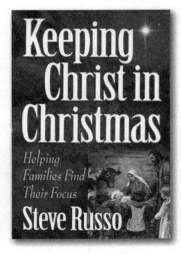

Do too many of your Christmas memories consist of frantic trips to the mall, frenzied entertaining, and an emphasis on Santa and presents? If you're longing to get back to a Christ centered Christmas and celebrate the holiday with joyful, family-oriented traditions, you'll be inspired by the practical ideas in this book for keeping Christ in Christmas.

This year will be refreshingly different as you focus on the real reason for the season! You'll discover how to...

- **keep your family focused on the birth of Christ**
- **avoid retail madness and the Christmas rush**
- **create fun family traditions that spread the season's joy**
- **talk to your children about Santa, angels, and other holiday customs**
- **share the promise of Christmas—Jesus—with those around you**

Creative ways to celebrate are interwoven with practical parenting advice to make this your ideal resource for enjoying the best Christmas ever!